How to
Blend
a Family

How to Blend a Family

CAROLYN JOHNSON

PYRANEE
BOOKS

Zondervan Publishing House
Grand Rapids, Michigan

HOW TO BLEND A FAMILY
Copyright © 1989 by Carolyn Johnson

Pyranee Books
are published by
Zondervan Publishing House
1415 Lake Dr., S.E.
Grand Rapids, MI 49506

Library of Congress Cataloging-in-Publication Data

Johnson, Carolyn, 1926–
    How to blend a family / by Carolyn Johnson.
       p. cm.
    "Pyranee books."
    ISBN 0-310-51241-7
    1. Stepfamilies—United States. 2. Remarriage—United States. I. Title.
HQ759.92.J64   1989   88–31534
646.7'8—dc19   CIP

MY "CASE HISTORIES" ARE COMPOSITES—REAL SITUATIONS AND REAL PEOPLE WITH THE DETAILS CHANGED ENOUGH TO PROTECT THEIR PRIVACY.

Edited by Nia Jones
Designed by Nia Jones

Printed in the United States of America

89 90 91 92 93 94 95 / EP / 10 9 8 7 6 5 4 3 2 1

Contents

Acknowledgments

My thanks to:

Carol, for professional guidance in the writing of this book.

Barbra, for reading every draft and cheering me on.

Harry, for all the breakfasts you cooked and for your loving encouragement.

Our children, for allowing me to tell our story.

All of the "blended" people who were generous enough to share their experiences with me.

Introduction

Families are not what they used to be.

Reruns of "Father Knows Best" and "Leave It to Beaver" are reminiscent of an era when the typical family consisted of a working father, a homemaker mother, and children who were related to each other and to both parents. These days, few families fit that idealistic profile.

Our family is one that the sociologists call "blended." My husband, Harry, and I created it when we picked up the pieces of our respective broken marriages and pledged to help each other get on with life. As we have blended our lives and those of our children, we have also mended our brokenness.

"Blended" is a nice-sounding term, but it suggests an accomplished state of unity and harmony that is unlikely to exist in the beginning of a second-chance marriage. The blending of persons is a process. That process led our family through a maze of obstacles without the guidelines for blended families that are available today.

If you are contemplating the blending of a family, or if you have already taken that precarious step and are finding more problems than you'd bargained for, we hope you will benefit from knowing some of the things that we have learned. Any of the insights we've achieved has come through and after our experience.

As Harry and I look back, we see many positive things about our own remarriage that helped us to survive the hard times. There were some negative aspects, too, that added unnecessarily to the problems of those years. Some of these could have been avoided had we known what to expect. Although each blended family is unique in itself, there are common pitfalls. Our family needed a trailblazer. Perhaps our story and those shared by other families like ours can fill that role for you.

Combination families, or stepfamilies, take many forms. In some, such as ours, both partners have full-time custody of their children. In others, one or more children visit regularly. Sometimes the stepmother or stepfather has had no previous experience with children. Some remarried couples have children of their own, which creates a his, my, and our combination. In every case, complex relationships, previously established life-styles, differing values, and healing wounds from the breakup of the first marriage are issues to be dealt with.

More than 45 percent of the people who get married these days have been married before. And more than half of those are the custodial parent of at least one child. In a third of the remarriages, both spouses have children from a previous marriage. This means that more than seven million children are transplanted into stepfamilies each year.

For these children to feel good about themselves and to grow up in a stable and secure home, we must help society accept and recognize blended families as respectable and positive alternatives to the conventional, nuclear family. Hopefully, this will come about when we, as blended families, see ourselves in an affirmative light and learn to take steps to insure a successfully blended family.

That is what this book is all about—*How to Blend a Family*.

1
A Different Kind of Family

W hen my father refused to walk me down the aisle a second time, he said he'd given me away once already and now I was on my own. His smile and the twinkle in his eye softened his words, but I felt his concern for me. My mother cried a lot. Our friends said we were crazy, and the world at large had little to say on the subject of second marriages.

In my starry-eyed youth I'd pledged my troth to a young man with whom I intended to spend my happily-ever-after life. We'd knelt before a priest and said forever words—promises that had echoed and died over the years. I came away from that marriage with sadness and guilt and a void in my life that ached to be filled.

Now in a resurgence of hope, I stood before another altar with another beloved. I was optimistic beyond reason that this time would be different. The fact that we planned to unite my four children and his five under one roof was a problem that our love and determination would solve, we naively reasoned.

Among the wedding guests, our friends and family suppressed their skepticism and wished us well. Our collective children, aged six to thirteen, covered their confusion with squirms and giggles and trusted the wisdom of their parents. As we recited our vows, Harry and I brought together the fragments of our broken dreams and laid them upon a new foundation of love and commitment.

Soul-searching and struggle had preceded this momentous decision to merge our families and our lives. Harry was forty-one and I was thirty-five—old enough to be reasonably cautious in affairs of the heart. Slightly addled by the excitement of our middle-age romance, we dared to dream of a second chance at marriage. We were both refugees of divorce, wounded and disappointed by the failure of our respective marriages, and we'd found reassurance and hope in our relationship.

I was the custodial parent of two girls, seven and thirteen, and two boys, nine and eleven. Harry's first family unit had crumbled so completely that his four boys, aged six, eight, ten, and thirteen, and twelve-year-old daughter had spent their last five years in foster homes, separated from one another and from their father. During that time, they had lost contact with their biological mother.

Harry wanted more than anything to reunite his family. I was his hope. And he was willing to father my children in exchange for my mothering his. Neither of us had any idea of the stressful adjustment ahead of us. After years of living in a bachelor apartment, Harry would be thrust into a household of wall-to-wall children. Adding Harry's children to mine would more than double my work load as a homemaker. Still, we were confident that we could meet the challenge.

"I know I can do it, Mom," I'd said, trying to reassure my distraught mother. "You know how much I love children."

"But, Carolyn," she'd protested, "you have more than enough to do now, with four of your own. And you won't be able to afford any help on a postal worker's salary."

"Sure, I'll have to make some changes—learn to cook in quantity and spend more time doing laundry. But look at how things were in the old days. People had big families then and thought nothing of it."

Mother shook her head and sighed. "There's a difference, honey. You'll see."

Those were prophetic words.

A Gathering of Strangers

My mother's words came back to haunt me. The family we created was different from any I had ever known. I had grown up in a Norman Rockwell era, in a world of nuclear families. Nearly all of my friends had one or two siblings, a homemaker-mother, and a father who went downtown to his place of business and returned home on the six o'clock commuter train. This was my model for adult life. After the dissolution of my first marriage, I drifted on uncharted seas. Security demanded that I reestablish the family unit and led me to marry again.

But our new family didn't *feel* like a family. We were a group of strangers, thrust together out of need, with few guidelines to help us understand the problems that soon surfaced and threatened to overwhelm us.

Where I had fantasized a calm and orderly beginning, chaos and confusion reigned. Where I had pictured myself as the patient, loving, and understanding mother of our brood, nervousness and fatigue sharpened my tongue and shortened my temper.

On our first evening together, we gathered at the dinner table—a slab of plywood that Harry had covered with laminated plastic and placed upon my old cherrywood drop-leaf to extend its length and width. The excitement of the day gave way to panic as I surveyed our motley crew. At the far end, our three youngest jockeyed for position on a picnic bench brought in from the backyard. The older boys elbowed one another and kicked an occasional shin under the table, while the big girls whispered and rolled eyes heavenward at the antics of their brothers.

Within minutes, the casserole that was supposed to feed fifteen was reduced to a streak of tomato sauce in the bottom of the Dutch oven. A few crumbs were all that remained of two loaves of freshly baked bread. My children's finicky appetites disappeared forever with the first breath of competition.

My mind reeled at the thought of this scene repeating itself over and over for years to come. *Who are all these people, and what am I doing here?* I thought to myself, as I tried to smile at Harry over the general confusion. Suddenly, even this husband that I had chosen seemed like a stranger.

That was my moment of truth, when fantasy and idealism deserted me and left reality in its wake. The reciting of our marriage vows had not automatically made us a family. And how on earth was I going to feed this mob tomorrow night and all the thousands of nights to come?

Is This for Real?

Many of us begin our second marriages with the idealistic dream of recreating the nuclear family. We want to be "real."

And "real" to me was a blood-related nucleus of people who belonged together by right of birth. The family was a strong base from which its individual members ventured into the world. Protected by their armor of security, they were tied by invisible safety ropes to one another and to home base. However, we were a group of people whose ties had unraveled and broken.

When I realized our status, I knew my choices were limited. I could accept the fact that we could never meet the requirements for "realness," or I could pretend. I chose to pretend and began our marriage by denying reality.

During the first few weeks of our merger, I took Harry's

two sick boys to the local medical clinic. "These are my sons," I said, refusing to use the dreaded "step" prefix. Moments later I was trapped by my evasion of the truth. I stammered with embarrassment when I admitted that I knew almost nothing of their medical history.

I will be their mother and love them all, I said to myself as I stood at the threshold of my new life. Love evaporated in the heat of anger and dissolved in tears of resentment and self-pity when I faced the reality of bickering, brawling stepchildren (not *mine*) whose overwhelming demands stole time and energy from the rightful claimants (*my* children). Forming bonds with the diverse personalities of my new family members seemed impossible. I was failing rapidly, and my self-esteem plummeted.

Day by day I was experiencing the truth of the wise words by Ruth Roosevelt and Jeanette Lofas (words that had not yet been written in that first winter of my discontent):

> The most pervasive myth in a stepmarriage is that the family should function as does a natural family. It doesn't. Classic mistake number one is to think that it will. It can't.[1]

We who enter a remarriage in a cloud of idealism will eventually see our dream castles collapse around us. Many of the disillusioned will give up and resolve the conflict with another divorce, compounding the injury to themselves and the children involved. Some of us will resign ourselves to an armed truce in a divided home where the two family units will live side-by-side in polite cooperation, where each parent takes responsibility for and provides emotional support to his own. The fortunate ones will relinquish their fantasies, stop trying to make their second families fit an impossible mold, and get on with life. They will accept their unique mix of individuals as a different kind of family, one with the potential for growing together into a happily blended family.

Under Reconstruction

For a long time I thought of our family as "prefab," like the house we eventually poured ourselves into. And in my secret heart, prefab meant a poor imitation of the real thing—a shaky structure of ill-fitting segments, hastily joined together to look like a solid building. That was my concept in those first difficult years, and we were like that. However, there are better descriptions of a combination family: reconstructed, recycled, synergistic, even amalgamated—each name coined in an attempt to replace the more common "stepfamily."

Although organizations like Stepfamily Association of America are working to promote respectability for the step-relationship, the stigma remains. Centuries of fairy tales have left their mark. Words like "cruel" and "wicked" echo in our memories.

Fitzhugh Dodson, renowned child psychologist, defines a stepfamily, or blended family, as a household unit where a stepchild (or children) lives or is a regular visitor. It is a family in which an extremely complex set of emotional relationships prevents easy harmony. In contrast, as Dr. Dodson says, "In biological families, as parents and children grow up together, emotional bonds are forged that help to smooth over the rough edges of the parents' deficiencies in parental skills."[2]

There are other terms to describe families like ours. John Hagedorn, LCA pastor and director of clinical services for Pastoral Counseling and Consultation Centers of Greater Washington, D.C., refers to us as "second families." "Blended," he says, "implies a sameness, a blurring of the individual persons and histories. Second families wish to retain all they have been, while creating something new."[3]

This may be true in some instances, but I would have found that theory hard to apply in our case. Harry and I were anxious to be different people and to move away from the destructive patterns that had led to failure in our first marriages.

Over time we did gradually assemble our "prefab" on the new foundation and adjust to one another. Now, after a quarter of a century of building relationships within our family structure, I like the idea that we are "blended." I think we've earned that title. We are individuals still, biologically related or not, but we have the common bond of a shared history.

In the combining of two existing family groups, at least one of which has suffered disruption and loss, there are bound to be feelings of jealousy and resentment. Under such circumstances, instant love is a fantasy.

Our Creator designed for us a lifelong, one-flesh union between one man and one woman—a relationship intended for our happiness and companionship, for procreation and protection of children, and for sexual fulfillment. Obviously, the high incidence of divorce and remarriage is not within the realm of God's perfect plan for His children. We fall far short of perfection—marriages are not made in heaven. They are entered into by fallible human beings in a world that has been clouded by sin since the serpent invaded the garden.

So we failed to meet God's highest standard the first time around. All is not lost. If we choose to try again, we can draw on our experiences, look to His ideal for us, and be optimistic about success in a second marriage.

Remarriage has been called the triumph of hope over experience. God has planted within man and woman a physical and emotional desire for one another. We are sexual and social beings. We long for intimacy—to know and be known, to love and be loved, to care and be cared for. Statistics show that most of us recover enough from a broken marriage to return to the altar with renewed hope.

One writer spoke of remarriage as the "drug-of-choice"

among those who seek escape from the pain and loneliness that follow a divorce. These individuals avoid coming to terms with their misery and rush into a substitute relationship. Statistics indicate that 60 percent of all such remarriages fail, many within the first three years.

What shall we do, then, when we have failed once at marriage and have found the hope and desire to try again? With the odds against us, do we have a right to subject ourselves and our children, our intended spouse and his children to the risk of further brokenness?

I think we do. God has given us a picture of what He intended the marriage relationship to be. He has given us the desire for intimacy with another, and He has given us the courage to try again. Most important, as in every phase of our existence, God in His compassion provides a bridge of forgiveness between our failures and our futures.

Only by the grace of God did Harry and I and our assorted children cling together until we began to be a family. We don't fit the conventional, biological image that existed in my girlhood dreams, nor are we another "Brady Bunch." We are a different kind of family—a uniquely interwoven group of individuals who have grown up together. We share a history now and a continuing commitment that have made us a family.

2
Leftover Pain

G rief, guilt, anger, fear, loss of self-esteem—all are painful products of broken marriages, whether interrupted by death or divorce.

Negative emotions are good in proper doses, but when we carry them into second marriages, they can hinder successful blending. Therefore, whatever the mix of emotions in that lonely time between marriages, they should be faced and resolved before we remarry. This takes time. Time to dull the sharp edges of painful memories and time to rebuild self-confidence and self-esteem. How can we help this process along?

Working through Grief

In the Book of Proverbs, "the teacher" says that "there is a time for everything, and a season for every activity under heaven" (cf. Eccl. 3:1). Time for weeping and mourning; time for laughing and dancing.

No matter what the circumstances were for your interrupted marriage, you have probably already discovered that you need a period in which to mourn the past before you are emotionally equipped to face the future.

When you marry for the first time, you leave your original family to begin a new family. You and your mate "become one flesh." This is a time for dancing and rejoicing. However, in the interval between divorce and remarriage most of us discover that we are suffering grief. This is just as natural and appropriate for the ending of a marriage by divorce as it is for the ending of marriage by death.

Elizabeth Kubler-Ross, in her studies of death and dying, has identified five stages of grief common to those facing death. These same stages—denial, anger, bargaining, depression, and acceptance—can be seen in those who suffer the devastating loss of a marriage. With the final "acceptance" phase, the period of mourning should come to an end, leaving us to deal with the other emotions.

Sometimes professional therapy is necessary before we reach the "acceptance" phase. It was for me. Crying jags and sleepless nights drove me to seek counseling. A few sessions with a family therapist helped me to unscramble my emotions and provided me with the reassurance I needed to cope with that difficult time.

But professional therapy, while very beneficial, may not be necessary for you, or even possible. Perhaps you can receive support from your extended family or your close friends. When you lose your spouse in death you learn to lean heavily on your friends and family members during your time of mourning. It is the same after divorce, if we allow ourselves to grieve.

A divorced person often denies himself the right and need to mourn his broken marriage, especially if he has been the instigator of the breakup. *I wanted out of the marriage,* he thinks. *How can I feel sorrow?* But if grief is suppressed, it is likely to reappear as a stumbling block to intimacy in a subsequent marriage.

The duration of the mourning period will be different in

each case. Often, it begins before the actual end of a relationship, as in the slow death of a loved one or the gradual breakdown of a marriage. In the process of grieving, the emotional ties to the lost person are gradually released. Only then can they be redirected toward another.

Remarriage after the death of a spouse is less likely to be encumbered by incomplete mourning. Sorrow comes easily to the one bereaved by death. Friends and family share the burden of grief, and the widowed one finds support as he works through his emotional pain. When he is ready to enter a new marriage, his greatest obstacle to happiness may be his tendency to idealize the lost love and to look upon the new mate as a replacement for the old.

An elderly friend, widowed for the second time after a delightful (in her words) fifteen years with her second husband, told me, "Even though my first marriage, with Melvin, was rockier and generally less satisfying than these last years with Stan, still I think of Mel as my 'real' husband and that marriage as my 'main' marriage—probably because we had the children together. Stan filled in where Mel left off."

Had she been widowed and remarried younger, while her children were still children, the shared experience of a growing family would probably have overshadowed her feelings about her second marriage.

Absolving Guilt

Carl and Connie are a young couple with his and her children. They married almost immediately after Connie's divorce was final.

"Carl and I met soon after I separated from Jack," Connie explained. "I was so caught up in the excitement of being in love again that I didn't face any of my negative feelings. I thought I could just close the door on the past and start fresh. Before the honeymoon was over, there were all kinds of ghosts coming between Carl and me. I couldn't tell him that I was thinking of my marriage to Jack and wondering if we should have tried harder.''

When Connie's marriage failed, she was hurt and disappointed, as most of us are. She had entered into marriage sincerely, even reverently. She happily agreed to forsake all others as she chose the one with whom she intended to spend the rest of her life. But, like most of us, she underestimated the difficulty of "loving and cherishing." For many people, "for better or worse" is mostly worse; "for richer or poorer" means only poorer; and sickness takes the place of health. We make promises beyond our human capabilities. Failing at one of her life's most important endeavors, Connie was left with deep feelings of remorse. Her sense of self-worth was diminished.

Guilt and a feeling of lowered self-esteem are weights that may threaten to sink a second marriage. Those negative emotions will overburden the delicate relationships within the blending family. They must be resolved to ensure a healthy start in a remarriage.

"I knew that Connie was on the rebound when we first started dating," Carl added. "But I felt like we had a good thing going and she'd forget him. It would have been easier for both of us if she'd gotten him out of her head before we got together. It didn't do much for my ego to know that she was mourning the past, when I wanted her to share in my excitement about our future."

Connie was unfair to her second family when she dragged the weight of the past into her remarriage. She was haunted as much by the pleasant times she remembered with Jack as by the misery they'd known together. No marriage is all bad, and ambivalent feelings about the ex-spouse are normal. Fortunately,

Connie realized that her ambivalence was harming her chances for happiness with Carl, and she sought counseling.

"Things worked out for us, of course," Connie said, snuggling closer to her husband. "I just wish I'd realized I needed some help before. My therapist showed me that I was so overwhelmed with guilt that I couldn't face the breakup of my marriage realistically. Some of my guilt was deserved, for sure, but part of the blame belonged on Jack's shoulders. When I understood and really believed that it takes two to make or break a marriage, I was able to forgive myself and look ahead."

Guilt is a devastating emotion. It burdens the heart and cripples the soul. It drains the energy from a productive life and blocks the free expression of affection to those around us. Guilt feelings may be justified or unfounded, as in the case of the battered wife who thinks she "deserves" her punishment. But whatever their source, they are the result of our own judgment against ourselves. Our standard of what is right or wrong has been violated, and we suffer.

In nearly every case of divorce, the participants come away with feelings of guilt. Wherever the greater share of blame for the dissolution of the marriage belongs, both partners have failed in their commitment. We have vowed to "love, honor, and obey," and we have broken that promise. We need to work through this guilt before we can give ourselves to another relationship. Depending upon the circumstances and the depth of feeling, this "working through" may require professional help, or it may happen naturally with the passing of time.

Gordon told about his difficulty in establishing a close relationship with his stepson. "It was almost as if I deliberately withheld any affection that I might have shown him," he said. A support group of other stepparents helped him to see what was happening. "I felt so guilty about leaving my own two sons with their mother that I couldn't allow myself to enjoy any kind of relationship with Richie, my stepson. To be buddy-buddy with him seemed disloyal to my boys. They were halfway across the country, and I figured, subconsciously at least, that if they couldn't have my attention, no one else should either.''

Unresolved guilt will prevent us from finding happiness in a remarriage, because, underneath, we feel that we don't deserve to be happy. In denying ourselves, we cheat everyone around us and spoil our chances for a successfully blended family.

Let me share with you some steps that were essential for me in overcoming my own guilt feelings:

1. I learned to accept things as they were, in spite of my sorrow and disappointment. My marriage had failed, and people were hurt. What *was* couldn't be changed.

2. I accepted part of the responsibility for the failure and stopped trying to rationalize it away. My guilt was deserved, but it was too heavy a burden to be carried for very long. In hanging onto it, I saw that I was forcing others to share my burden.

3. I came to realize that I was an imperfect human being in the process of growing and that growth can be painful.

4. I became determined to learn from past mistakes and focus on the future.

5. I understood, finally, God's provision for sin in Jesus Christ and was able to forgive myself as He forgave me.

This was a slow process for me, and guilt followed me into my second marriage. Taking the first four steps helped me to cope with my remorse, but not until Jesus entered my life with His loving gift of forgiveness did I shed the last of my burden.

Coping with Anger

Anger is another natural emotional response to divorce. If we think that our former spouse deserves most of the blame for our broken marriage, we feel victimized, and we are angry. If we have been weighed down by guilt for our own part in the breakup, we have a need to justify ourselves. We look for and magnify the faults in our former partner in an effort to relieve our own emotional pain. As we remember every hurtful act, our anger increases.

"I really don't think I could have gotten through my divorce if I hadn't been able to work up some anger toward Jack," Connie remarked. "I'd been a doormat for so long— always *felt* the responsibility for everything that went wrong— that it took some time away from Jack to see things objectively. "In that marriage I was like the whipping boy. Oh, not that he ever was physically abusive, but if the hot water heater sprung a leak or the vacuum broke down he'd act like it was all my fault.

"I remember one day in particular. We were getting ready to go on a little vacation, and I'd been running around doing last minute chores and supervising our three preschoolers. I'd come in with a load of laundry to fold and pack, neglecting to close the kitchen door behind me. When Jack came home (He'd been across the street playing cards.), he opened the front door, and the kitchen door slammed shut in the sudden draft, shattering the glass panes. He was furious. He raved at me and said that I was stupid not to know that would happen, and I believed him. There was always some logic in his accusation. Anyway, he was mad, and I was hurt, and the beginning of our vacation was spoiled. When I look back on incidents like that I can feel rightfully angry at his intolerance, and that anger helps me counteract the guilt."

The tendency to place the total responsibility for a broken marriage on the other person is as unhealthy as accepting all the blame. If we can take a realistic look at what went wrong, we will have taken an important step toward the future. For to understand yesterday's mistakes helps us live more successfully today. But we must be careful not to get bogged down in "if onlys." Reliving the past is not an option.

Although anger turned outward can be healthier than bottled-up resentment, it is a negative emotion and can compound our problems. If we haven't been able to express our feelings at the proper time to the rightful recipient, they are apt to lie in wait for the first excuse to overflow. Anger can leak out in spurts of irritability and sarcasm or explode in an emotional tirade. In either case, the target will usually be an inappropriate one—a friend, a child, or a prospective spouse.

The Bible seems to demand the impossible of us when we read "in your anger do not sin" (Eph. 4:26). God knows we will have occasion to be angry, and He wants us to learn to deal with our emotions without hurting ourselves or others. Harbored and fed, anger becomes resentment, and resentment nearly always goes hand-in-hand with self-pity.

Peace at any price is an unhealthy bargain. Innocent bystanders often pay the price when we seethe and smolder inside rather than admit our feelings when we are offended. If you can express anger in a controlled manner to your offender, it is wise to do so. If confronting him would cause more problems than the offense merits, talking it out with a pastor or trusted friend is a good alternative.

Daniel talked about his resentment over his broken marriage. "I was so angry when I came home to find the note from my wife, saying that she was leaving me and the kids to 'find herself.' I hadn't made any close friends since our last move, and my parents and brothers lived out of state, so I had no one to talk to. My bitterness turned me into a tyrant at the office and a real grouch at home.

"My sons were having a hard enough time as it was, and my foul temper made it worse for them. I was furious at Charlene for hurting them, but I wasn't helping the situation with my attitude.

"Then, when one of the boys got into trouble at school, I got called in to talk to the school counselor. I had to tell him what was going on at home, and that turned out to be a blessing in disguise. That guy helped me realize what I was doing to myself and the kids. I called my brother and unloaded to him for an hour, long distance, and then I sat down and wrote Charlene a long letter, telling her just what I thought of her running out on us. I tore up the first draft and wrote it over again, leaving out the really spiteful parts, but I felt better for having gotten it all down in black and white.

"After the boys and I had a few more sessions with the school counselor, we were all in a lot better shape."

Daniel had been unable to express his initial anger to Charlene because she'd left without a confrontation, and his pride had kept him from confiding in anyone within his circle of acquaintances.

"The idea of going to a 'shrink' never occurred to me," Daniel added, "but now I can see the value of just talking things out. I'm not out of the woods yet, by any means. I still have a lot of bitterness about what's happened. But I've stopped banging my head against a stone wall and started facing reality. My main concern is for the boys, and the best thing I can do for them is to keep my own head on straight."

Overcoming Fear

"Someone told me that divorce was like an amputation," Evelyn Brown said, "and that exactly described my feelings. Suddenly I felt less than whole, unbalanced—the emotional equivalent, I guess, of being one-legged. I'd gotten rid of something that was hurting me, but still, I didn't know how to function. I was definitely 'handicapped' by my loss, and I was terrified.''

Fear of the unknown future threatens to paralyze many newly single individuals, especially those who married young, before they'd had time or opportunity to establish independent identities. Even when there is welcome relief from the constant strain of an unhappy relationship, as there often is, a sense of loss and insecurity marks the end of a marriage.

Here are some fears that undermine the confidence of a newly single mother:

- Will I be able to manage financially?
- What do I need to know about servicing the car?
- Are the children and I still covered by health insurance?

Her former partner will have his own battles.

- How am I supposed to afford the rent on this place and pay child support, too?
- Do the kids miss me? Are they taking their mother's side in our breakup?
- How do I fill the lonely hours, now that my family is gone?

These fears and many more arise as we face the unknown future.

''All of a sudden I didn't know who I was or where I belonged,'' said Judy. ''I'd gone from being part of my childhood family to being half of a couple, and now I was alone. It was a real identity crisis. I had the kids, of course, but I needed another adult to share the day-by-day responsibilities of life. And I was nearly desperate for company. Suddenly everyone I knew was either married or involved in the 'singles' scene—a lifestyle that didn't appeal to me and certainly wasn't a place for my girls. I felt isolated and afraid of being alone forever.''

An incident that stands out in my own memory occurred

shortly after my separation from my first husband. A former babysitter was being married and delighted the children with an invitation to her wedding. I was fixing the girls' hair when the boys—eight and ten at the time—came into the bedroom for help with their cuff links and ties. I had never learned to tie a man's tie and hadn't the faintest idea where to begin. I was feeling estranged from my neighbors at that time, but I had to swallow my pride and send my sons across the street for help.

It was a little thing, but it made me realize how helpless I was in a lot of areas. If I couldn't manage a boy's tie, how could I survive a real crisis? If I couldn't ask my neighbors for help, who could I call on in an emergency? I began to feel very apprehensive about what might lay ahead.

Another crippling fear, in addition to the unknown future, has to do with relationships. Our most intimate bond with another person has broken, and we are wounded in the process. Is it worth the risk, we wonder, to establish another close relationship, to become vulnerable enough to love and be loved again? If we have been rejected, we fear another rejection; if we have been disappointed in our expectations, we shy away from situations where we may suffer further letdown. We may put on a mask of aloofness as a buffer between our emotional bruises and those around us, thereby choosing the safety of loneliness over the risk of intimacy.

Coolness and indifference can be protective coverings for our past injuries, but they work against our natural desires for love and companionship. Every individual has a deep basic need to belong, and belonging involves interaction with other persons. We need a place in the world, among people, that is uniquely ours.

Fortunately, these fears that are expressed in questions such as "What do I do now?"; "Who am I?"; and "Where do I belong?'' gradually diminish with time and positive action. We cope. We adjust. We heal.

Restoring Self-Esteem

If we are fortunate, we will have completed the healing process before we marry again. We will have shed our tears, resolved our guilt, quenched our anger, and overcome our fears. But, more often, we enter our second marriages with emotional leftovers from the past and tenderness in areas that will affect our relationships with our new families.

"For a long time, I reacted to everything that Roger said as if Ted, my former husband, were saying it," Cynthia recalled. "When Ted asked, 'What have you been doing all day?' he asked it with a sneer and a sidelong glance at any unfinished chores around the house—you know, dishes in the sink or laundry on the sofa waiting to be folded. It was undisguised criticism, and my response was defensiveness. But when Roger asks about my day, he really wants to know what I've been doing. I know that, but just hearing those familiar words triggers my defenses, and I get angry and sarcastic."

Cynthia smiled as she went on. "Luckily, Roger was sensitive to my sore spot and learned to rephrase that question. There were other things, too, but I gradually realized that Roger didn't deserve to take the brunt of my bitterness. As a matter of fact, as I did some soul searching and saw my own shortcomings in my first marriage, my bitterness disappeared. Roger and Ted are different personalities, and my relationship with Roger is entirely different from what I had with Ted in my first marriage."

Cynthia took an important step in her own healing process by looking inward and examining her contribution to the failure of her first marriage. Roger's easygoing disposition helped her regain confidence and allowed her to lower her defenses.

Loss of self-esteem is almost universal among divorced persons. Sometimes, as in Cynthia's case, it is restored gradually within the context of a supportive relationship. In my own case, facing and coping successfully with a crisis or two began to build my confidence.

My friend Liz shared her own secrets of recovery after an ego-deflating divorce. "I'd been battling my husband's efforts to undermine my confidence for years, but my defense was mostly bluff, like a small dog with a big bark. After we separated, his words kept coming back, and I began to wonder if he'd been right all along.

"Through a girlfriend, I got involved with one of those 'direct sales' training programs. At their meetings all the emphasis was on building our self-confidence. 'You can be whatever you want to be,' they told us. I soaked up their philosophy like a dry sponge, and it helped me immeasurably. From there I read every 'positive thinking' book I could get my hands on. I even took an assertiveness training course.

"One day I decided I'd been in my dead-end job long enough and walked out. The next morning the boss was on my doorstep, offering me a better job with higher pay. I was well qualified for the more responsible position, and he'd always known it, but my lack of confidence had shown. And he was perfectly willing to take advantage of my weakness.

"The job change was a turning point for me. I didn't need to pump myself up any longer with clever slogans and manufactured enthusiasm. I was proving myself in a challenging job and making enough money to support myself. And I began to see that my husband's need to put me down stemmed from his own lack of self-esteem and had nothing to do with me."

It's not easy to feel good about yourself after the failure of a marriage, but take heart. You can reinforce the healing power of time by taking some positive steps to restore your confidence and recreate a healthy self-image. Here are some suggestions that have helped others.

1. **Accentuate the positive.** Take a personal inventory; concentrate on your strengths and abilities. Remember any praise or compliments you've received in the past. If you've been called a wonderful cook, bake a pie and enjoy your talent.

2. **Associate with cheerful people.** There are "uppers" and "downers" among your friends and acquaintances. Stick with the people who build you up and leave you smiling.

3. **Set yourself some achievable goals.** Strive for a feeling of accomplishment at the end of a day. Tackle a job you've been avoiding—painting the outdoor furniture or reorganizing your desk. Don't set yourself up for failure by trying to do everything in one day.

4. **Learn something new.** Sign up for an exercise class or a course in conversational French. Learn to crochet or make Christmas decorations.

5. **Do something for someone else.** Volunteer for Meals on Wheels or take flowers to a shut-in. Practice giving out some of that good cheer that you look for in others.

All of these will help to bolster your self-esteem and bridge the chasm of loneliness and discouragement that follows a broken marriage.

Securing the Innocent

These emotional hurdles—grief, anger, fear, and loss of self-esteem—are not limited to the adult victims of divorce. Our children suffer the same emotions and follow a similar path in their transition from one family to another.

Mourning for the absent parent is healthy and natural. One expert saw incomplete mourning by children as a major psychological block in forming relationships with stepparents.

Guilt is a common reaction in children whose parents have divorced. According to experts, this is especially true in the 6–12 age group. Often a child may feel that he has in some way caused his mother and father to separate. "If I were a good boy," he reasons, "my father wouldn't have left me."

Anger toward one or both parents may accompany or follow guilt feelings. This anger is sometimes suppressed until it is suddenly vented upon a prospective stepparent. The child's secure and familiar world has fallen apart, and he, too, experiences fear.

His biological parents are in the best position to help him work through this difficult time. If they can show a united front in their love for their child and their concern for his welfare, even though the marriage is over, they will provide the security necessary for his adjustment to the divorce and remarriage.

Not every child of divorced parents is doomed to develop emotional problems. Child psychologists say that it is not the "broken home" that is to blame for emotional disturbance in a child but the way his parents handle their separation and divorce. Children can cope with the transitions involved in a marriage break-up if they're not burdened with too many changes too quickly. The more things in their lives that can remain the same, the better. They can recover from their hurt, which is not to be denied, if they have help from the people they love.

Calling on the Body

Not only do victims of broken families suffer the pain of these emotional by-products, they also must cope with the stigma of divorce that still exists, especially in Christian communities. Too often the divorced person suddenly finds himself or herself rejected by friends and neighbors, and life becomes very lonely.

We count on the understanding and support of our church families during most of the crises in our lives—illness, accident, financial hardship, or the death of a loved one. Divorce seems to be an exception to the disasters worthy of the church's ministry. Carole Sanderson Streeter confirms this.

> The church's lack of attention to the matter of forgiveness is evidenced by the very low level of church attendance among newly divorced people who normally go to church and by the fact that so many divorced people change churches. It is also evidenced by the lack of recovery and growth in many divorced people.[1]

Rather than face the cool reception and rather obvious disapproval of our formerly friendly congregations, many of us opt to stay home or visit a series of other churches where no one knows us or our circumstances. We put on our "happy" masks and shield our aching hearts from our new acquaintances. In this way we protect ourselves from any hope of the loving support that we so desperately need.

Fortunately, this is not always the case. There are church families like Amy Ross Mumford's, who writes about her own experience.

> I'm sure there are churches today who do pull in the welcome mat when a newly singled adult appears at their doors. Many books and articles are written relating personal experiences that bear out this fact. Divorced persons have been embarrassed, rejected, barred from service, and even been asked to produce the divorce decree to prove the reason for the divorce.
>
> This is sad. I'm thankful that I have not found this to be true in my life. I feel loved, respected, supported and welcome. If I did not—I would quietly steal away and look for a church who would welcome me with open arms in Christian love.

She rejects the idea of being relegated to a special "singles" group.

> I don't want a "place" made for me where I am set apart as
> if I were some unusual species requiring special treatment. I
> want to belong to my church. The whole church. Not just a
> "place" in it.[2]

An encouraging trend is the emergence of support groups within the church that minister to those going through the trauma of separation and divorce. First United Methodist Church in Gulfport, Mississippi sponsors "The Broken Rainbow," a program "where the children whose parents are divorced or separated may come to discuss their emotions and needs." An additional program, "Just Me and the Kids," addresses the needs of the newly single parent. In Santa Barbara, California, Trinity Church of the Nazarene provides "Divorce Alliance," a program "designed to lessen the hurts and to help meet the needs of those going through the separation, divorce, and recovery process."

There are churches who give lip service to forgiveness and acceptance of those whose first marriages have failed, but they go only halfway in their ministry. Many divorced-remarried persons suffer what one writer called "endless moral cruelty" in their churches. They may be allowed to be members and to participate in Holy Communion, but they may not teach a Sunday school class or sing in the choir. This tradition leaves them in the shadow of adultery. If God fully accepts them into the body of Christ, shouldn't they be fully accepted into the church body?

Even in the more liberal churches, divorced people experience more than their share of pain. Marjorie, a recently divorced member of a large and active church, shared her pain,

This has been a humiliating experience. It wouldn't have been so bad if Scott had left town or changed churches or at least stayed single for a decent interval, but here he sits every Sunday with his new bride. I've been singing with this choir for years, and it means too much to me to quit, just when I need things to fill my time more than ever. So I look down at my former husband and the New Mrs. W. smiling up from the center of the congregation, and I die inside. It's ironic. I'm singing hymns about Christian love and feeling nothing but hatred in my heart.

I'll say this though. People have been wonderful. Maybe some Christians would think that our church is too liberal, but all I see is the forgiveness that Christ taught. It must be tough for Scott and his wife, too, but they seem to have had as much support from members of our church as I have. Otherwise they couldn't keep coming. Gradually, I'm learning to hold my head up and respond to the kindness of my Christian family.

Divorce within the church is an unhappy reality. It is evidence of the sinful condition that we share with humanity. Perhaps it is time we stand our ground and stay within our church families, mustering courage enough to share our pain with our Christian brothers and sisters. Given a chance to see our deep need for their understanding, I'd like to think they will choose to reach out to us in the kind of healing ministry that they so generously bestow upon other hurting members.

Looking Ahead

The past cannot be left entirely behind. It will follow us in memory, in habit patterns, and (after divorce) in our dealings with an ex-spouse. In most cases, the children of a first marriage will tie their biological parents together for many years. Child support payments, visitation arrangements, and shared interest makes the first marriage part of the fabric of the second. This is a significant area of difference between the stepfamily and the nuclear family.

> Divorce, though it cancels the partnership of man and wife, never severs their relationship entirely. When two people have once been so joined, it is little wonder they are never fully separated afterwards. The experiences of marriage have created a million microscopic electrical contacts in the brain, and no judge's signature on a piece of paper can undo that multitude of connections; many of them, indeed, will endure until the current itself is turned off.[3]

Past experience leaves its mark. However, it is obvious that both the adult and child victims of divorce need to distance themselves emotionally from the failed marriage before they can be psychologically ready for another intimate alliance. Nearly all of us have found it impossible to close the door all the way on the past, but we can come to terms with our negative feelings and shift our attention to present reality.

We can make the most of today, accepting and rising above our circumstances, and look with optimism and a sense of adventure toward the uncharted future.

3
Love Is Lovelier

*L*ove is lovelier the second time around." Those words, made popular by Frank Sinatra in the early sixties, echoed in my reawakened heart. Falling in love at midlife proved just as spine-tingling and mind-addling as it had been at sixteen, but it was a lot less convenient.

To be a single mother of four young children is serious business. I had no time for frivolity and little room in my days for romance. But reason deserted me. Love burst in like the sun after a storm and warmed all the cold and empty corners of my life. Grief had spent itself; hope was a balm to soothe my wounded soul.

Every year thousands of us who share the lonely world of the formerly married fall in love again. If we are fortunate, that love will be genuine, and it may lead to a successful second-chance marriage.

Love is the first prerequisite for such a challenge. It takes a special kind of love to combine families—a love that goes beyond the romantic, pulse-throbbing infatuation that may come too easily in the vulnerable aftermath of a broken marriage. Genuine marriage-worthy love, encompasses mutual respect and trust. In a blending family it must be strong enough to compete with the parent-child bonds that each spouse brings to the marriage and expansive enough to include children not our own. Unfortunately, men and women in crisis are in a poor position to judge the lasting quality of their emotions.

Our God-given need to love and be loved is the basis for every romantic alliance. Often, however, we substitute emotional or economic needs for the qualities that make up lasting love. These practical needs are so powerful that they can obliterate all reason so that only failure and tragedy can follow.

Most statistics indicate that the divorce rate for second marriages is higher than that for first marriages. The odds are against us. Many couples realize, after their second attempts at marriage have floundered and failed, that it was need—emotional or economic—rather than love that led them to remarry. It is easy to be confused by the rekindling of romance.

In Love or in Need?

When Harry and I met, we were both lonely and insecure. My self-confidence and self-esteem had shriveled and died along with my marriage. The void in my life left an ache, like the dry socket of an extracted tooth. My heart yearned for an intimate relationship with another adult. Many of my close friends had drifted away, and I no longer fit into their couples' world. The only women with whom I seemed to have anything in common were one or two divorcees whose lifestyles didn't appeal to me.

My children were small, and I was untrained for anything besides housewifery. Lack of courage, as well as lack of skill, kept me from approaching the employment agencies. Support checks from my former husband kept food on the table and a lid on my pride.

I felt the stigma and the isolation of divorce. I didn't like being a divorcee with a boyfriend. When Harry came to visit, we were both ill at ease, sensing that my formerly friendly neighbors disapproved of our relationship. (The term "relationship" these days, is often used when referring to a live-in, sleep-together arrangement; but twenty-five years ago we were protected from that temptation by the more conventional, less liberal standards of that era.)

Our religious convictions did not go far beyond the Golden Rule. So security, for me, lay in the replacement of a marriage, an unbroken home, and a two-parent family. Harry, too, was hungry for love and companionship, and his greatest desire was to reunite his scattered family. His children were in foster homes and seemed destined to remain there until he found a wife who would be willing to mother them. Our needs were both practical and emotional. They combined to create a powerful force that hastened our decision to marry. It could have been a disaster, but by the grace of God it wasn't. Need might have propelled us to the altar, but I don't believe it would have kept us in a marriage without love.

Had we been Christians, we would have had the advantage of a firm foundation and biblical guidelines for our marriage. As I look back now, I believe that the Lord saw us—His prodigal children—coming from afar and protected us in many ways.

Economics—A Poor Foundation

Marriages based on economics are on shaky ground. Sally and Frank's marriage was one that had such an incentive.

"I have to admit," Sally confided, "that our reasons for getting married were as much economical as emotional. With my job as a checker at the grocery store, I was barely making the rent payment. Babysitters were expensive and unreliable, and so was my old car. Hal was good about the child support checks, but it just wasn't enough to make ends meet.

"Frank's son, Paul, was a teenager—too old for a baby-sitter but too young, really, to be without supervision, especially when Frank had business calls to make in the evening. Frank owned his own architectural firm, but he found himself having to choose between neglecting it or neglecting his son. He chose in Paul's favor, and his business suffered.

"It was obvious that if we joined forces both of us would benefit. I could work part-time and create a stable home situation for my own children and Paul, and Frank could spend more time with his business, which had great potential.

"Good grief, how naive we were! I had no idea how to deal with a teenager. I think everyone ought to work into that gradually, don't you? The financial situation improved for my kids and me, but Frank suddenly had twice the expenses and three times the distraction he'd had before. There was a long, hard period of adjustment for us, and I thank God we made it. But a marriage isn't a business arrangement. I wouldn't recommend that anyone go into a second marriage for reasons of economy."

Courtship—A Family Affair

In the ideal courtship—the kind God had in mind for us—a young man and young woman have *time* to come to know and understand each other. Moreover, they have the energy of youth and the approval of family and friends. However, second-time-around romances often have none of these props and are far from serene. Where children are involved, the road to the altar can be an obstacle course.

Consider this scenario: Steve invites Sue to go to dinner and a movie. Sue has promised to transport little boys to a Cub Scout meeting and help her sixth grader with her science project. "I'll be free on Friday night," she tells Steve. But that's the night he's arranged to pick up his son for the weekend. "Tell you what," he says agreeably, "I'll take Randy home Sunday afternoon, and then we can take in that art show in the park and try that new restaurant afterward." Sue stifles a groan as she reminds him that Sunday is her mother's birthday and she's expected for dinner. They finally settle on an afternoon of miniature golf with all the children, followed by hamburgers at Happy Burger.

"Steve and I played a lot of miniature golf," Sue recalls. "To be honest, a lot of times I'd look at him over the heads of our three children with lust in my heart and desire in my flesh. We were like a couple of giddy adolescents, stealing kisses behind the hippopotamus on the fifth tee and plotting time to be alone together.

"In a way, the kids protected us from developing a too-intimate relationship. We may have acted like teenagers, but we were, after all, sexually mature adults. In another way, our children probably were the cause of our marrying more quickly than was wise. Finding time to be together was such a hassle. Getting married removed that source of stress. But neither Steve nor I had put the past behind us. We were still in the healing stage after our divorces. We had to muddle through some things after we were married that we should have dealt with before."

The frustrations of midlife courtship, including sexual tension, can cause friction and misunderstanding. The couple feels the pressure of their individual responsibilities to children, jobs, and household duties. As they have developed different lifestyles in separate worlds, they have also acquired obligations to extended family and friends.

Responsibilities from the past must be honored, not swept under the rug. Necessary separations will test their relationship, which is good, but the resulting frustrations can also serve to push the couple into an ill-advised marriage. The sources of irritation and disagreement should be faced and worked out during the courtship period, or they live on to compound the problems inherent in second marriages.

When Harry and I fell in love and began to date, I allowed him to absorb most of my attention. Although I was usually at home, caring for my children, thoughts of him and our flourishing romance addled my brain. I heaped all my emotional dependency upon him, to the exclusion of others in my life—my friends, my parents, and even my children.

Harry and I couldn't be together as often as we would have liked, but we spent a lot of time on the telephone. One day we were deep in conversation when my eight-year-old asked me for permission to carve his pumpkin. Without thinking, I handed him a knife from the kitchen drawer and turned back to the phone. Moments later Tommy burst through the door crying, blood gushing from deep cuts in his fingers. Undergoing hours of surgery to repair severed nerves and tendons, he paid the price for my inattention, as I sat under my mantle of guilt in the hospital waiting room.

After that, we redefined our priorities. Harry was fond of my children, and he began to fill a new role in their lives. He entered more and more into our family life, taking part in our holiday celebrations, excursions to the park, and Saturday afternoon gardening projects. This gave us a chance to know each other under ordinary circumstances, and it lifted part of the burden of child care from my shoulders. He wasn't, at this point, trying to be a father to them (They had a good relationship with their own father.) but he was their friend, and they responded to his efforts.

Love Me, Love My Kids

Perhaps the phrase "forsaking all others" should be written out of a second wedding ceremony. When children are involved, as they are in a blending family, they must *not* be forsaken, physically or emotionally. If they are to be part of the restructured household, they must be grafted in the marriage bond, partakers of the promise "to love and to cherish."

"I made a mistake," one man said, "when I thought I could keep my children and my new wife separated. Emotionally I just couldn't compartmentalize my life. I was the noncustodial parent, but when I didn't make my kids part of my new household, they felt I'd cut them off from what was really important to me. Oh, they came to visit, but we allowed them to feel like outsiders. On the weekends they were there, we discontinued our usual lifestyle, as we might for houseguests, and concentrated on special activities for them. Their stepsisters were polite, but they resented giving up their accustomed family routine to entertain my kids.

"I see now that they should have been given a chance to know Adele and her girls before we were married. I understood the importance of 'courting' Adele's daughters while I was dating their mother, but I didn't think it mattered much if my kids liked my new family. After all, we weren't going to have them living with us."

Sometimes custody arrangements don't work out as planned. When Sheila and Bob were married, they planned to leave Bob's teenaged son, Brad, in his mother's custody, but when she married again, there was friction between Brad and his new stepfather. He turned more and more to his father, and his visits to that household became more frequent until, finally, he moved in for the entire school year. Bob was pleased and flattered, but Sheila felt pushed aside. Had they created more opportunity for Brad and Sheila to get acquainted before the marriage, everyone would have been more comfortable.

Predictable jealousy often develops between a child and his

prospective stepparent. This can be a base for future trouble, if it is allowed to go unresolved before the marriage.

"I felt like I had to fight for Martha's time," said Ed, a forty-year-old stepfather of three. "It was either her night to help at Awana or one of her kids was home from school with the mumps. Between the usual childhood diseases and their allergies, they were sick a lot during that winter after we met. I knew they couldn't help it, and I had no right to resent them, but I did.

"One evening I'd gone to see Martha and needed to talk about something that was going on with my own daughter. I waited patiently until she got her kids down for the night, since I knew I couldn't expect her attention as long as they were around. I even dried and put away the dishes she'd left in the drainer, made us a pot of hot chocolate, and brought in a log for the fireplace, as I anticipated a couple of hours alone with her. I knew she cared about me and would understand my worry over Betsy."

"Oh, poor Ed," Martha groaned, as her husband recalled painful memories, "that was a bad time for us."

"We'd just gotten settled down," Ed continued, "and I was explaining how Betsy's grades had taken a nosedive since her mother moved them into another school district, and how she'd gotten rebellious at home, and how she'd cried and told me how unhappy she was the last time I'd taken her out. Suddenly I realized that Martha had stopped listening and was looking over my shoulder at something. There stood Billy, her nine-year-old, wheezing and gasping for breath with another asthma attack. I hate to admit what a jerk I was, but I'm telling you like it happened. I jumped up, grabbed my coat, and stomped out, shouting at Martha that next time I'd make an appointment. And poor Billy. I hissed at him as I walked by—told him he was a spoiled brat who couldn't stand to see his mother have a few minutes to herself. An hour later I felt awful."

"He called to apologize the next morning," Martha added, "but I didn't even want to talk to him at that point. Our relationship just didn't seem worth the trouble. Ed's behavior that night seemed out of character, but I began to wonder if I really knew him. Later he called Billy and apologized to him. Billy'd been really crushed because Ed had always been so nice to him, but he was more willing to forgive him than I was.

"Ed didn't realize how discouraging it was for me. I was working part-time and having a struggle to keep up with everything. My kids were demanding more attention than ever, and I found myself resenting them for that. I resented Ed, too, for putting pressure on me, although he was usually pretty understanding."

"I respected Martha for the very things she did that upset me," Ed went on. "She put her responsibility to her children first, and that's the way it should have been. I admired her for that and for her ability to cope with a difficult situation. Her ex-husband had literally disappeared from the scene, so she had all the responsibility for her kids. She had some money from the divorce settlement and a small trust fund from an inheritance, but she had to work part-time to make ends meet. Martha budgeted carefully, and I saw her sacrifice some of her personal needs, so that she could be home when the kids were out of school."

"And I appreciated Ed's consideration for us. He was understanding and unselfish with his time, nearly always. I don't know how many times he changed his plans for us, to fix something around my house or take one of the kids somewhere. Liking the kind of man he was came before falling in love, and I couldn't let that one incident spoil everything."

Growing into Love

Ed and Martha had each accepted their roles as single parents. They had been divorced for enough years to have put their unhappy marriages behind them. Theirs was not a rebound romance or a desperate grasping for a replacement of an intimate relationship. They had developed coping skills, and these skills had given them renewed confidence and self-esteem. They had been attracted to each other, become friends, and then grown— rather than fallen—into love.

If you suddenly "fall" into something, it is apt to be a romantic infatuation, rather than love. Sometimes an infatuation will develop into a love that stands the test of time. When it does, it will have taken the route of shared interests and growing consideration for the feelings and desires of the beloved.

People grow into love over a period of time, seeing each other in a variety of situations and under many circumstances. Dwight Hervey Small, in his *Design for Christian Marriage,* says,

> A couple in love will talk about many common interests outside themselves, which become at the same time a part of themselves. They turn their attention outward to the world they live in as well as inward to their feelings about each other. They do not merely get off by themselves; they move together into a full sharing of rich values and experiences they find outside themselves. They do not look only at each other, but they look together at the larger life around them, discovering a range of common interests, shared friendships, and challenging tasks. They face together the important problems with which human beings must cope in a mature relationship to life. They look together at all of the issues involved in taking their place responsibly in the world as a unit of two and perhaps more. They love with their minds and wills and purposes as well as with their hearts. And because they love with their minds, their emotions

achieve new depth and meaning and constancy. Their love takes on a spiritual quality as they recognize their love as a gift from God. They recognize that marriage shall be an undertaking in the presence of God as well as a venture with each other. Thus, an infinite dimension is added to their shared life. Love is woven into a pattern of living, and thus is begun a true and solid identification.[1]

If you "fall" into love, be suspicious. You may have fallen into, or stumbled onto, a temporary prop for your shaky self-confidence. Your new romance may be nothing deeper than an answer to your loneliness, and it may bring reassurance to your fears about being able to love and be loved again. If it is genuine love, it will grow in depth and in quality, becoming stronger with time. Genuine love, not infatuation, must be the foundation for a successfully blended family.

"With Both Feet on the Ground"

To point out the various practical reasons that couples enter into second marriages is not to say that these marital mergers are cold and calculating. A measure of passion has tipped the scales in every decision to remarry. But as everyone who has been married once knows, passion cools to a simmer as the honeymoon period gives way to everyday life.

A second-time-around marriage *can* be lovelier than the first, with our heads out of the clouds and both feet on the ground.

Love is washing dirty socks and other unromantic acts of service. If there is to be any hope of success in a second marriage, we must commit to a deeper kind of love, one that puts the welfare of others ahead of our own. We need to carefully and prayerfully examine our motives for remarrying and plumb the depth of the love we feel for our prospective spouse. The Bible gives us a blueprint for love in 1 Corinthians 13:4–7.

> Love is patient, love is kind. It does not envy, it does not
> boast, it is not proud. It is not rude, it is not self-seeking, it
> is not easily angered, it keeps no record of wrongs. Love
> does not delight in evil but rejoices with the truth. It always
> protects, always trusts, always hopes, always perseveres.

Wow! With that kind of love we would have stayed in our
first marriage, wouldn't we? That is God's standard and our goal.
My inadequate love contributed to the failure of my marriage. I
always knew that, even before I became a Christian. When I
came to know the Lord, I was dismayed to see how far I had
drifted from God's will for my life. Knowing Him now, I can
allow Him to fill me with His love and hope that some of it
overflows upon those around me.

Love at first sight may be merely wishful thinking. Second
sight is the clearer vision that comes with time and a venture into
intimacy as we trust one another enough to uncover our souls
and share our lives in open, honest communication.

Harry and I talked a lot. We'd spent half our lives apart in
separate worlds and we had an insatiable desire to know
everything about each other. We spent time sitting over coffee in
my kitchen, sharing future dreams and past hurts and failures. It
was a kind of therapy for both of us, and our habit of
communication became a vital part of our marriage. We became
friends, learning to trust and respect each other, before we were
catapulted into the difficult beginnings of our family-blending.
We found that sharing the same values was essential in dealing
with each other's children.

Norman Wright, in his book *Fulfilled Marriage,* says,

> One of the greatest disasters to hit marriage is thinking of
> the spouse as a lover and sexual partner without seeing him
> or her as potentially the greatest friend one could ever have.
> Marriage is a form of friendship—it is a gift from God.[2]

More than once we hear marriage referred to as a "gift from God." How infinitely precious, then, is the realization that God has blessed us with a second gift. Like a forgiving, compassionate parent whose child has lost or destroyed the original gift, He offers us a second chance. Our hearts must sing with joy and gratitude. It is pure grace. Now we can echo the words of the apostle Paul.

> Brothers, I do not consider myself yet to have taken hold of it. But one thing I do: Forgetting what is behind and straining toward what is ahead, I press on toward the goal to win the prize for which God has called me heavenward in Christ Jesus (Phil. 3:13–14).

We will be a giant step ahead if we can shine the light of God's Word on our own lives before we remarry.

4
Starting Over

T his isn't working out like I expected. We'll never be a real family, so what's the use?" As I mumbled these words to myself in the early days of my second marriage, I was discouraged, and came dangerously close to sharing them with the rest of the family. I had not yet aligned my expectations with reality.

Nuclear families develop slowly; however, beginning with a marriage between two people whose pasts are comparatively uncomplicated. The marriage relationship usually has a chance to grow before the first child appears, and that child's bond with his parents is secured before another sibling joins the family unit. The blood connection gives each child an equal claim to a significant position within the family.

In a blended family, however, individuals are brought together in a marriage that will be difficult at best, and the resulting relationships must be dealt with simultaneously and immediately. In that way, blended families are intrinsically different from nuclear families.

We can never quite start over. We drag bits of the past into our new relationships. We never completely sever ties to a former spouse with whom we have had children. We need to give up any expectation that we can erase our first marriages as if they had never happened and recreate the nuclear family. Threads of sadness from the past are interwoven with happiness and hopes for the future.

But God is the author of new beginnings. Although a remarriage can never duplicate that first one-flesh union, it can be a positive alternative. The first step, as we look toward the future, is to put aside old myths and commonly-held stereotypes about stepfamilies.

Because blended families, like all others, are made up of unique individuals, no two family units—large, small, nuclear, blended or extended—will have the same style or flavor. Each group will develop its own methods of relating to one another and to the outside world. And within every family unit, each member is constantly in flux, changing ways of coping with life stress and adjusting interpersonal relationships. To compare our blended family to a nuclear family is an exercise in frustration. Realizing that our family is one of a kind will keep us from mentally assigning ourselves to some second-class category, discouraged before we begin.

That, of course, is hindsight wisdom. Looking back, I can identify with Elizabeth Einstein, who said of her herself, "My notion that step was bad, negative, second best, let me wear the mantle of victim and yield responsibility for the direction of my life."[1] I understand that feeling. It was behind the defeatist attitude that caused me to hang my head and mumble a vague explanation when someone would ask why our children were unnaturally close in age or had different surnames.

In combining families we bring together two separate family systems whose behavior patterns have developed over the years and are not easily abolished. New family members have vastly different ideas about food, mealtimes, living space, privacy, responsibilities, and leisure-time activities. What we did that was taken for granted within our smaller family unit may no longer work in the blending family.

Habits are hard to break or change. Moreover, after being traumatized by the upheaval of divorce and remarriage, we are apt to resist further adjustment. We are weary of change. As we grope to establish a firm footing in our new family, we can expect to have feelings of insecurity and moments of panic, wondering if we'll survive the first months of restructuring.

To enlarge our living area, we recently had our small house remodeled. What we thought would be a simple project became a major undertaking. On the expanding side of the house, it was necessary to tear back the roof and ceiling, leaving half the house exposed to the elements. Solid plaster walls were replaced with plasterboard, and still serviceable carpet had to be discarded. Construction dust and debris coated the trees and shrubs, littered the patio, and filtered through to the remaining part of the house.

For weeks we lived in discomfort and confusion. After the project was completed, Harry and I worked hard to restore order and cleanliness, but the reconstruction had left its mark. Seams in the ceiling, scars on the woodwork, and uneven places in the expanded foundation overshadowed the luxury of our added floor space. Our house didn't seem like home. It took months for us to "grow into" our unaccustomed elbow room, to enjoy the convenience and become blind to the flaws.

We had had unrealistic expectations about our remodeling, just as many of us do about our second marriages. We had pictured the final result without counting the cost.

Nothing worthwhile comes without cost, as the words of our Lord remind us.

> Suppose one of you wants to build a tower. Will he not first
> sit down and estimate the cost to see if he has enough

money to complete it? For if he lays the foundation and is not able to finish it, everyone who sees it will ridicule him, saying, "This fellow began to build and was not able to finish" (Luke 14:28–30).

The Wedding

Ceremonies celebrate beginnings and give society's sanction to a solemnized event. Ordinarily, a lot of thought and planning go into that day on which we celebrate our second wedding. In our first wedding we might have worried about how many attendants we should have or who would feel left out. The second time around, however, the bridesmaid and best man take second place to children of the bride and groom. Should the children of both families be included in the wedding celebration?

My friend Gloria was married for a second time after a long and stormy first marriage. She and the husband of her youth were products of the sixties, and he was a casualty of the drug culture. She never lost faith that he would be delivered from his addiction, and her religious convictions precluded any thought of divorce. Six children were born to this marriage, and it was for the protection of these children that Gloria finally sought a separation. Their marriage ended in the psychiatric ward of the county hospital, where her husband died of a drug overdose.

Gloria and her children were set free at last. Her family and friends rejoiced when, two years later, a new love entered her life. Gloria's children encouraged her to marry again and wanted to take part in the wedding ceremony. They had begun the mourning period for their father long before his actual death, and they were ready to accept another man into their lives and into their home.

In our culture, ceremonies help us to make transitions from one life stage to another. We march from grade school to junior high to the strains of "Pomp and Circumstance," and we're transported from single life to marriage as we speak words of love and commitment in a ritualistic setting. Since blending families gain cohesion with every shared experience, the wedding ceremony can be the first significant memory in the life of the new family.

Harry and I didn't want to be married among strangers or by an impersonal justice of the peace. We wanted to share our happiness with family and close friends, and we counted on their presence as a symbol of their approval and support. We weren't church-goers, but we decided to be married in a church, and we chose one at random. We wanted to recite our vows before God, and we thought it more likely that He would be in church than at city hall.

It never occurred to us to be married without our children present. We wondered, on the last day, if we had taken too much for granted. Chris, my eleven-year-old, drooped around all day, looking like he was coming down with something. Joan, Harry's twelve-year-old, called to say that she had too much homework to come to the wedding. We realized then that they were acting out a last-minute protest of more change in their young lives— change directed by adults and over which they had no control.

Should we have consulted our children about our plans to marry, rather than announcing our intentions to them after our decision? We thought not. To include them in the decision-making process seemed too great a burden for such young minds. Our relationship had developed gradually, and our engagement came as no surprise to anyone. We made firm plans for the future and then announced them to our children, hoping for but not asking for their approval. To ask would have seemed like an admission of doubt on our parts, and it would have put them in a position of more responsibility than they were prepared to handle. We hoped that our excitement and enthusiasm would be contagious enough to gain their cooperation.

I think our positive attitude was reassuring. We acted as if we knew what we were doing, and the children trusted our show of confidence. On the other hand, I believe we should have given them opportunity to voice their negative feelings, reassuring them that it was okay to *have* such feelings. When Chris and Joan reacted on our wedding day, we were unprepared and too involved with our own interests to help. Later I understood that they were watching their private dreams crumble forever. For Joan, it was the fantasy of someday making a home for her father and brothers; for Chris, it was the hope that his father and I would be reunited. Theirs were only two of the unexpressed dreams in the hearts of our children. Perhaps Harry and I didn't have the understanding or the emotional energy to deal with them.

In spite of any reluctance, however, all nine boys and girls were polished and present at our wedding to watch my knees tremble and Harry's voice go hoarse with nervousness as we spoke our vows. Ours was more than a marriage between one man and one woman. It was the merger of two families. I'm glad we were all there to share in our beginning.

Some years after our marriage, I read this statement, attributed to Amy Vanderbilt, "It is poor taste for young children of the first marriage to even attend the marriage of either parent the second time, if a divorce has taken place." Many people would agree with her, but one young couple of my acquaintance included their children—his and hers—in their wedding *and* honeymoon plans. Her twelve-year-old son acted as best man for his stepfather, and his seven-year-old daughter was flower girl. After the wedding, parents and children sailed to the Caribbean for a family honeymoon.

"Why not?" asked the bride. "Our children are part of the blended family that Alex and I created when we married. Shouldn't they have been part of the celebration that marked the beginning of our lives together? Listening to our vows made them more aware of our commitment to each other and to their future with us.''

She has a point. Aren't we sending the wrong message when we "protect" our children from this experience by excluding them? I believe their participation in this rite of passage—one that will have a profound effect upon their young lives—can only add to their sense of stability and security.

Elliot and Ginny's children were young adults when their parents married. Two were willing and eager to participate in the wedding ceremony, another agreed to "put in an appearance" at the reception, and another refused to have anything to do with the marriage.

"Finally," Elliot said, "we canceled all the arrangements we'd made for a small church wedding and a garden reception and flew to Hawaii. The kids that approved of our marriage had a small party for us afterward, but Heidi, one of Ginny's daughters, 'had other plans.' It's okay. We'd like them all to be happy for us, but we have to accept it the way it is. Heidi's young, and she may see things differently someday."

The presence of other adults—grandparents, uncles, aunts, and long-time friends—helps to put a stamp of approval on the second marriage. Although my parents were less than thrilled about my remarriage, they came to our wedding out of loyalty, and their coming made a difference to my children. They loved and respected their grandparents, and to have them in attendance at our wedding was reassuring.

Our children have shared the sorrow and emotional turmoil caused by the dissolution of our first marriages. By inviting them to share in the celebration of our new beginning, we can help them to release the past and accept our plans for their futures.

Someplace like Home

After we have shaken the rice from our shoes, our first priority is to establish a home for the children of our blending family. Every remarrying parent wants to make the transition from one family situation to another as painless as possible.

The choice of a place to live together deserves careful consideration and prayer. Chances are, whatever we do, some- one—or perhaps everyone—will feel displaced. Although mov- ing from a familiar home and neighborhood will cause further upheaval in a child's life, in most cases the advantages of starting the new family in a neutral setting far outweigh the difficulties. Where stepsiblings will live together, as in our case, it is almost essential.

One family counselor observed that when two sets of children are brought together by a new marriage, one set regards itself as the "main family" and the other as the subfamily. The determining factor, she said, is whose house becomes the family's home.

Before Harry and I combined our families, he was living in a bachelor apartment and his children were in foster homes. My four children and I were occupying most of the available space in my house. Our choices were limited. We needed a house big enough for us all, and we needed to live within range of a job for Harry and a good elementary school for the children. Forced to move, it seemed better to find an entirely new area for our newly combined family.

We chose the beautiful and rural Santa Ynez Valley for our future home, and Harry was able to obtain a job transfer within the postal department. Several hundred miles would separate us from old friends and familiar territory, but we would all share in the adventure. Together we'd face the challenge of making new friends and adjusting to the unfamiliar rural setting.

While our home was being built, we rented a three-bedroom house on a barren hillside. Three children filled each of the bedrooms, Harry and I slept in the family room, and cartons from former households were stacked along the walls, waiting to be unpacked in our new house. Our crowded conditions and lack of privacy grated on everyone's nerves. The rains came, marooning us in a sea of mud. The bare floors and walls of our six-room prison echoed with the trapped energy of nine displaced children.

"Do they have to make so much racket?" Harry asked almost daily.

"It's the boys' boots," I said, referring to the black high-tops that we'd bought to withstand the local terrain. "Maybe we should have gotten them rubber soles."

That winter was the most difficult period in our family's history. But our circumstances created an adventure that we were forced to share and provided us with lifelong memories. Sharing, we found, is the catalyst that begins to blend people into families.

Not every new family is able to begin on neutral ground, as we did. After Sally married Frank, she and her three children moved into Frank's larger house.

"My children immediately felt like intruders," Sally said. "Paul, Frank's teenage son, gave up his privacy to share a room with my ten-year-old David. Paul had been used to having the house to himself most of the day, and now his stepbrother and two little stepsisters seemed ever-present.

"Of course Paul resented me and my kids. I would have felt the same way at fifteen. We'd invaded his turf, as he would say, and he rebelled. I resented him, too, for making my kids feel unwelcome. It caused friction between Frank and me, and the whole family got off to a bad start.

"When Frank and I opened our eyes to Paul's needs, we

took some steps to correct the problem. I explained to David that Paul's side of their bedroom was absolutely out of bounds to him and his friends, and the girls were forbidden to *ever* enter the boys' room without an invitation. When Paul saw that they respected his right to privacy, he was a lot nicer to them. He still didn't have enough space for a teenager, so he and Frank designed and built him a room off the garage with an outside entrance. I was afraid Paul might feel more displaced than ever, but he loved it.

"I suppose we could have avoided a lot of problems if we'd moved into a home new to us all," Sally added. "But we were lucky to be financially able to remodel Frank's house to fit our expanded family. I guess most remarrying couples aren't so fortunate."

The fair division of space is only one disadvantage of moving into one family's existing home. Memories can haunt old and new residents alike. Paul's mother had been dead for several years before his father remarried, but he still had memories of her kneading bread in the kitchen and brushing her hair at her dressing table in the master bedroom.

"I like Sally okay," he said, "but it hurt sometimes to see her in my mom's place."

Frank's next-door neighbor had been his deceased wife's closest friend. Sally knew this and always felt that she was on trial. "I was trying so hard to be worthy of my place as wife, mother, friend, and neighbor—it was like being a substitute teacher with someone else's lesson plan. I was miserable until I just gave up and decided to be myself."

As each blending family needs a home, each individual family member needs a place within that home where he can feel comfortable and secure. The nesting instinct is prevalent within all of us. We cling to the familiar as we venture into new surroundings and circumstances.

In the beginning, none of our children had much of a "place." For seven-year-old Nancy, squashed between two big sisters in a king-size bed, security was her own pillow and a battered stuffed dog. For the older girls, unlimited use of the bathroom mirror and one drawer each for cosmetics and curlers helped to counteract the strangeness. A ten-year-old might want nothing more than a place to set up his electric train; an older teenager, a corner for his records and stereo.

A Place of Belonging

Our need for a place extends beyond the material. Our deepest need is to belong to *someone*. While the parents of the blended family are actively fulfilling this need, the child may feel that he belongs to no one. He has experienced the loss of one of his parents by death or divorce. In the interim between marriages, he often has become closer and more dependent upon the remaining parent. When a stepparent enters the scene, the child may feel further loss, as he finds himself competing for the attention of his custodial parent.

Twelve-year-old Jeremy was a case in point. When his mother and father, Betty and Lloyd, separated, he experienced all the emotions expected of a boy his age. He suffered with guilt at his imagined part in sending his father away; he mourned the loss of his role model and fishing companion; and he cowered under the sudden responsibility of being "the man of the house." On the other hand, he felt pleased at having his mother to himself and enjoyed the special, close relationship that developed between them. When George, his stepfather-to-be, began to rob him of some of his mother's attention, he was resentful and rebellious. Like most children, he'd thought of his parents as asexual beings, and the displays of affection between George and Betty confused and disturbed him. When Betty agreed to marry

George, Jeremy took her decision as a personal defeat, judging that he'd lost the contest for his mother's affection.

The family moved into George's house, where Jeremy found added competition in an older stepsister. Betty's efforts to win the girl's friendship resulted in creating more insecurity for Jeremy. When he returned home from school to an uncomfortably strange house, he would often stand hesitantly at the front door, wondering if he should ring the doorbell. Once inside, his "Hi, I'm home!" might go unheard by his mother and stepsister, engrossed in "girl talk" behind the kitchen door. He found no opening for the familiar, after-school camaraderie he'd had with Betty before. George stood by, hoping for an opportunity to begin a relationship with his stepson, but Jeremy had built a wall between himself and the man he judged to be the cause of his unhappiness.

Jeremy desperately needed a place of belonging in the new family structure. That was his first priority. Until that requirement was filled, he could not let go of his dependence on his mother and begin to build relationships with the new people in his life.

Every parent wishes for his or her child to feel happy and secure within the new family structure. The single greatest challenge and responsibility facing the parents of the blending family is the welfare of the children whose lives have been disrupted by change. An understanding of the needs of all children will help us in our attempts to provide security for our own. Every child has basic needs. They are especially important to children of changing family structures.

 • **Children need to know where they belong and what will happen to them.**

Harry and I tried to prepare our children ahead of time for some of the changes to come in their lives. We took pictures of the valley we'd chosen for our home and drew floor plans of the house we planned to build. We visited the elementary school to pave the way for our youngsters and brought back enthusiastic reports of small-town friendliness and menus from the cafeteria. We subscribed to the local paper for several months before our move, and, when we finally followed the moving van into town, things looked reassuringly familiar to our children.

Those were the little things that we were able to do to diminish the initial strangeness of our new beginning. Our efforts probably alleviated the stress of the actual blending process.

● **A child needs to know that his relationship with his biological parent is constant and secure.**

It is easy to be so caught up in the demands of our newly structured family and its maze of relationships that we neglect or take for granted our bonds with our natural children. Betty unwittingly did that with Jeremy.

"I was so anxious to get on well with Alicia, George's daughter, that I kind of put Jeremy on hold. I thought he was just being rebellious, but now I see that he was feeling really deserted. When we got back to some of our old habits, like our after-school routine, he was a different kid."

● **A child needs physical space for himself and his treasures, and he needs reassurance that his territory is respected by others in the family.**

Helping to establish that special "off limits" place for each child, as Frank and Sally did for Paul, is something parents *can* do. Their efforts will prove their concern for their children's individual needs.

● **As far as possible, a child's privileges and responsibilities should stay the same within the newly formed family. He needs to know that he is a useful and valuable member of the family and that he is appreciated for his contribution.**

A child's sense of his own worth—his self-esteem—is closely connected to his feeling of competence. For a stepfather to suddenly jump in and take over the trash-emptying or lawn-mowing chores that a boy has considered his own (though he may have complained loudly about doing them) will diminish his confidence. A more productive move on the part of the new parent would be to enlist the child's help in a family project where he can learn a new skill.

Change—even positive change—unsettles anyone's feelings of security and well-being. But constant adaptation to new people and situations is part of life. Teaching our children to be flexible matures and develops them as persons. In a remarriage, everyone may fumble around for a time searching for a comfortable "place" within the family, fitting into new circumstances and learning to cope with new relationships. In the process everyone experiences an inner emotional stretching. The resulting growth will help us to cope with the stress to come.

Defining Roles

Getting off to a good start in any new relationship takes patience, compassion, and sensitivity. Sometimes the role we will play in our restructured family is not clearly defined.

We stood in the narthex of the church, watching the bride and groom as they greeted the last of their wedding guests. At the very end of the line the bride's nine-year-old son waited patiently to attract the attention of the man his mother had married. The groom saw him at last and bent down to hear the whispered question: "Are you my daddy now?" I was standing close enough to hear Jimmy's urgent tone of voice and our friend's answer.

"In a way," he said, choosing his words carefully. "But I'd a lot rather be your pal."

I'd known Jimmy long enough to understand the yearning behind his question. His biological, alcoholic father had kept him at an emotional distance for the first years of his life and then disappeared completely. The little boy had waited for a letter or a phone call or any word at all from his father. After a while he'd stopped mentioning his name and no longer jumped up in eager anticipation at the sound of a car in the driveway. But his heart had a vacant place, and he wanted a dad—not a pal.

Our friend, the groom, was being considerate, thinking it presumptuous to expect to fill a natural father's shoes, but the invitation was there, and the door was open. Fortunately for them both, Jimmy persisted. His caring stepfather, given the advantage of time and physical closeness to his stepson, was sensitive and responsive to Jimmy's needs. He was more than glad to fill the role of father in his new family.

More often, a child will resist the efforts of his stepparent to take the place of his biological parent. Some stepmothers, contrary to their negative reputation, are apt to come on too strong in their hurry to make up for lost nurturing. Ann recalled her beginnings with her stepdaughter Emily.

"I felt so sorry for this awkward little thirteen-year-old who'd come into my life along with Neil. I think I had visions of turning Emily into a princess overnight. Our first outing together was a day in the city, shopping for stylish clothes and having her hair professionally cut. I thought it was a great success—came home bubbling to Neil about how adorable she looked. He noticed that Emily wasn't as enthusiastic about her transformation as I was and mentioned it later. He really jolted me when he said, 'Maybe Emily wants you to like her just as she is.'

"Of course he was right. It took me a while to realize that I was thinking more of myself than of Emily. I'd never had a daughter, and I think I was regressing back to my doll-playing days. You know how a little girl will dress up her doll and take her out for her friends to admire? I was playing mommy, and Emily was my real live doll. I didn't stop to think that she already had a mother—one who thought she was terrific, stringy hair and all. Even if she had needed a mother, I was rushing things.''

Getting off to a good start in our new family, we need to proceed slowly, getting to know our mate's children as people. If we can look beneath the surface of their evolving personalities and try to understand their unique needs, we will build a stronger foundation for future relationships with our stepchildren.

It usually works best for a stepparent to be a friend first and parent last. The time frame will depend upon the willingness of both parent and child to move on to a more intimate relationship. Here are some questions you might ask yourself as you begin to interact with your stepchild.

- What kind of relationship does my stepchild have with each of his biological parents?
- Can I somehow be an instrument of peace—not discord—within these relationships?
- Can I resist competing with (or "putting down") the absent parent and compliment his influence by bringing something of value to this child's growing-up years?
- Can I look beneath the sometimes obnoxious behavior of a hurting child to see the hidden needs?
- Can I allow my stepchild to withhold part of himself from me, accepting the fact that we will never achieve the brand of intimacy that begins with the parent-child bonding of infancy?

Dad, Harry, or Hey You?

My children first knew my future husband as Harry, their mother's friend. After we were married and he became the resident father-figure, I asked them if they would mind calling him "Dad." They complied without a murmur of dissent, reserving "Daddy" for their biological father.

I've read since that stepchildren should not be asked to call their stepparents "Mom" or "Dad." (Where were these authorities on blended families twenty-five years ago, when I needed them?) At the time, it seemed the logical solution to the naming problems in our family, and I think it fit our situation. When there are two sets of children under one roof, as there were in ours, it seemed unnecessarily divisive to have my children calling Harry by his first name, while his children called him "Dad," and his children calling me Carolyn, while mine referred to me as "Mom."

For everyone to use the same names for our blending family members gave us one more area of mutuality. I think there may have been an interval of awkwardness, when "hey, you" took precedence over anything else, but we were soon comfortable with the familial terms.

Karin, stepmother to two teenagers, relates a different experience. "At first, Pete's kids came to stay with us just for the summers, and it was during those periods that we established our 'friend' relationship. They were pretty grown up when they moved in permanently, and they had no inclination to call me anything but 'Karin.' I was barely old enough to be their mother, anyway, and 'Mom' would have sounded strange, coming from them."

"What about your own daughters," I asked her. "They were just nine and eleven when you and Pete got together."

"I know," Karin answered. "But, as I've told you, our 'getting together' in the beginning was just that—without benefit of marriage. We weren't Christians then. Everything felt so temporary. Later, when Christ became part of our lives and we got married, Pete was just 'Pete' to the girls. Their biological father has never been around, and they certainly think of Pete as a father, but it would have seemed kind of phony to them to start calling him 'Dad.' ' "

Karin's daughters adore their stepfather. His given name is said with as much affection as any more familiar term. In their case, as in many others, they did what came naturally, and everyone is comfortable with the family vocabulary.

Reverend John Hagedorn feels that the "step" terminology is awkward and often inappropriate, since the "step" prefix comes from an old English word that means "bereaved" or "orphaned." He says, "I ask the members of the newly created family to refer to themselves relationally. 'This is Paul, my wife's son'; 'I'm John, Steve's mother's husband'; 'This is Mary, she's Mom's husband's daughter.' "[2] Perhaps these terms are more accurate and explanatory, but such formality would never have fit with my own "real family" image.

When Harry went to a teacher's conference and said, "I'm Harry Johnson, Nancy Hobson's Dad," I think the circumstances of their relationship were obvious. In identifying himself as Nancy's "Dad," instead of Nancy's mother's husband, he was claiming her as his responsibility.

Naming decisions, when there is any question, should be left up to the children. If a child is reluctant to call his stepparent "Mom" or "Dad," his feelings should be respected.

Easy Does It

Veteran stepparents agree that the wisest approach to the newly blended family is to proceed slowly. We are faced with our own preconceived ideas and the prejudice of others; we are challenged with complicated relationships; and we are sadly lacking in ground rules. It will take time for us to discover who we are as a family and how we can live together comfortably, with benefit to us all.

Statistics tell us that the odds of successfully blending a family are against us. The divorce rate for remarriage is given as 44–60 percent. Many remarriages dissolve within three to five years. Some will endure in mutual misery. The interaction of family members during the first months and years will either strengthen or weaken the foundation of a new family.

All of us have made glaring mistakes and would call back the past, if we could, to smooth out the wrinkles in our beginning years. We tried too hard or not hard enough. We bungled our attempts to be good parents to our spouse's children. We were horrified at our lack of love and compassion for these children that we had pledged to nurture. We've been hurt and disappointed when our sincerest efforts were met with rebuff.

We stepparents tend to be more guilt-ridden over past mistakes than natural parents, perhaps because we expect more of ourselves. Many of us have pictured ourselves as rescuers and fantasized about our heroism, to the exclusion of focusing upon our stepchild's unique needs. It was obvious to Ann that Emily needed help with her clothes and her hair, but she almost missed seeing Emily's deeper and more subtle need for acceptance as a person.

One university study shows that it takes stepfamilies an average of four to seven years to stabilize emotionally. Many of us are giving up too soon, discouraged and disheartened by unexpected difficulties and unrealistic expectations.

I can remember those first months on our muddy hill, standing in the shower after everyone had gone to bed. Hot tears mixed with the warm spray on my face. My body ached from the physical exertion of caring for our brood, and the sounds of another chaotic day still echoed in my head. Thoughts of running away drifted through my mind, but there was nowhere to go.

Optimism returned with a bright winter morning when our little troop trudged down the road to the school bus.

5
Tending the Flame

*E*xperts agree that maintenance of the couple relationship is the first prerequisite for success of the blending family. But the building and maintaining of a relationship takes time, and we never seemed to have enough. The very mechanics of moving households, transferring schools, locating a pediatrician, setting up bank accounts, and finding our way around our new community used up the extra minutes in our days. Harry was thrust into a new job, and I was overwhelmed with my role as cook and caretaker for a family of eleven. Not satisfied with all this newness and eager for more living space, we began construction of our new home and waged almost daily battles with an unreliable contractor.

When Harry came home in the evening, tired and needing my undivided attention, I was preparing dinner, supervising baths, and helping with homework. Later, with the dishes done and children tucked into bed, some immediate problem would demand our attention, crowding out the little personal things that we'd looked forward to sharing with one another.

Where our personalities meshed, our biological "clocks" did not. I was a night person, clinging to a habit I'd established when my children were babies and the late hours were the only ones available for sewing or catching up on the ironing. Harry had midwestern farm blood and loved to be on hand for the first light of day. Modern research suggests that a person's biological clock is to be respected, but our different rhythms robbed us of precious time together.

In her article, "Guidelines to Happy Families," Gladys M. Hunt says,

> The first ingredient for a happy family is a well-put-together mother and father. They will not be perfect, but they are working at evicting the dragons from their souls and have established a loving relationship together that gives their children a sense of security. Within the circle of home there is *safety, safety* because there is genuine love, open communication, and a way of handling conflict that is well defined and acceptable.[1]

Like many prospective stepparents, we anticipated the challenge of forming and nurturing ties with our spouse's children, but we took for granted the continuing flow of love and understanding between ourselves.

Having pledged our love and loyalty to one another before God and other significant people, we were secure in our commitment. We were grown-up people, with feet planted more firmly on the ground than in our first youthful marriages. We had grown close with time and had genuine concern and compassion for one another. Certainly there would be problems ahead in the blending of our families, but our relationship with each other was assured, wasn't it? Of course it wasn't. We should have known from past experience that a marriage relationship left to survive without nourishment will die. Our marriage vows were only the beginning. We needed to constantly reaffirm our commitment, which threatened to cool in the wake of post-honeymoon reality. Dwight Hervey Small puts it well,

Marriage cannot be less than a total commitment, and such commitments must be accepted on the basis of the realization that each life will be laid open to a new range of hurts and burdens not possible previously. As each one shares in all that touches the other, life takes on a double risk and responsibility.[2]

Fanning the Sparks of Communication

Communication is the lifeblood of every relationship. It exists in some form as long as there is physical proximity between two people. The quality of communication within a marriage can strengthen a fragile bond or weaken a solid one. We exchange messages by touch, facial expression, body language, action, attitude, and spoken word. Conversation is not necessarily communication. Conversation can deteriorate into meaningless small talk where intervals of tense silence hide unspoken hurts and frustrations.

During our courtship Harry and I loved to sit over coffee, sharing our innermost thoughts and hurrying to fill in the missing pieces of our lives. We thought, then, that we'd go on talking— communicating—forever. However, in the beginning stages of our marriage, we were hard pressed to finish a sentence without interruption. Our long, intimate talks became a thing of the past. Communication, as a priority, was quickly shoved aside by the urgency of our day-to-day life.

In the beginning of our marriage we stumbled over another block to our previously open communication. We were inclined to deny or ignore any problems that arose between us. Jeanne Thompson Varnell, writing in *Christian Home,* explains,

> Because blended families are formed against a background of hurt and failure, they tend to cover over conflicts, fearing that their expression will lead to more hurt and separation. This false harmony often expresses itself in the sentiment

"Let's not rock the boat this time." It is difficult to help
blended families look at this, but down the line it usually has
a crippling, eroding effect on the relationship.[3]

Our experience bears that out. There were few enough
peaceful intervals in our turbulent household, and neither of us
wanted to disturb these times by raising controversial subjects.
A resentment pushed below the surface, we found, was often a
seed planted for future misunderstanding.

In a second marriage, there are areas of communication
that present hazards unknown in a first marriage. Touchiest of
these is in the "your kids/my kids" department. It is hard to say
to a beloved spouse, "Your son is vulgar and crude, and if I had
my druthers I wouldn't want my son to associate with him." It is
painful to hear from one who has pretended to love your
children, "Your daughter is a spoiled brat." We know that
words like that hurt, and we don't need to say them to each
other. We have to learn to discuss our combined children in love
and with sensitivity to our spouse's feelings.

"What advice would you give someone starting out as we
did?" I asked my husband on our silver wedding anniversary.
"What did we do to stay in love?"

"I think our communication was the main thing," Harry
answered. "I don't mean just talking, but listening to each other.
You listened to me, even when you weren't particularly
interested."

Harry is good at remembering the positive things in our
marriage. There were times, I know, when he had less than his
share of my attention. The willingness to listen is a gift we can
give each other. Listening with an open heart brings understanding, and with understanding comes compassion and the ability to
"hear between the lines."

"Another thing," he said, "a couple should look beyond

the honeymoon and realize it won't be easy. I'm not sure I did that, but I recommend it."

"I think it's just as important to look beyond the bad times," I said, remembering the tears in the shower.

Looking back on our twenty-five years, neither of us could say, "This was the thing we did that made the difference." Our marriage, like any other, was shaped and molded by trial and error. Perhaps, in the beginning, we hung on because there was no honorable escape from the overwhelming obligation we'd taken on when we combined the broken pieces of our families. But Harry was right; communication kept our relationship alive.

Taming the Fiery Tongue

While sparks of communication need to be fanned, destructive words need to be controlled.

Harry reminded me—after an outburst of temper in which I'd hurled bitter words at the nearest target, him—that words once spoken are irretrievable and can leave lasting scars. James, in his letter to the twelve tribes, said,

> The tongue also is a fire, a world of evil among the parts of the body. It corrupts the whole person, sets the whole course of his life on fire, and is itself set on fire by hell (James 3:6).

When I've remembered the power of a fiery tongue, I've spared others from undeserved pain and myself from remorse. Long after an emotional storm has passed, harsh words can stick like splinters in our memories.

There are bound to be moments of déjà vu in a second marriage. "I thought this time would be different, but you're just as unreasonable (insensitive, selfish, inconsiderate, etc.) as he was!" Or, conversely, from the widow who continues to idealize the late spouse, "*He* would never have done that!" There is always a dimension of surprise, "Oh, I didn't know you were like this!" And times when one partner will look at the other with the condemning thought, "Now I understand why your first marriage fell apart!"

We like to think that our first marriages failed because of the shortcomings or weaknesses of our former partner. In the new marriage we begin to see our own feet of clay. Disillusionment with ourselves, with our spouses, and with marriage in general is a common hurdle for remarrieds. Once overcome, second-marriage bonding can take place upon a foundation of realism.

Unspoken resentments must be resolved in some manner, or they will drive wedges into every small crack of the couple bond. We need to be honest with ourselves and allow our negative feelings to come to the surface, but we don't need to let them overflow onto the one we have vowed to love and cherish. Pastoral counseling or the willing ear of a close friend is a wise alternative.

I found a kindred soul in our new community, and she became a trusted confidant. Upon Leslie's broad shoulders I heaped my frustrations, large and small, and from her generous heart I received sustaining encouragement. I consider it no coincidence that, shortly before our chance meeting, I'd written these words in my tear-stained journal:

> It's no use. I can see now that this isn't going to work. What kind of ego made me think I could take on a family like this? It isn't just the work, which is never done, but the atmosphere. None of the kids seems happy, and Harry is so wrapped up in his own problems at the job that he has little time for me. When I do try to talk to him about some of my frustrations (usually about one of *his* kids) he gets upset and thinks I'm being partial to my own. I suppose I am. Of course I am. How can I not be partial when I've known and

understood them since they were babies? He doesn't understand about maternal love. Besides, they treat me with consideration. *His* don't seem to care about my feelings at all—the boys, anyway. Sometimes I think they hate me. Probably Joan doesn't really like me either. She puts on such a cheery front about everything that it's hard to tell. I know she must think that I'm hard on her brothers, and I am, sometimes, but I just can't seem to relate to them. I feel like running away, but where would I go? I've made an awful mistake, and I'll just have to live with it. The worst part is that everyone else will have to live with it, too.

I'm so lonely. The phone never rings. If only I had a friend to talk to. . . .

God sent me Leslie. Ours was one of those rare, instant friendships, begun because our daughters needed help in making pom-poms for their eighth grade cheerleading squad. In our first conversation, over strips of blue and white crepe paper, there was that spark of recognition that happens between two people who have traveled some of the same paths in life. For the first time since my marriage, I was able to express my doubts and fears aloud. Leslie listened, nodded in understanding, and spoke words of encouragement that made a difference in my life.

Echoes of the Past

Nostalgia for the past can cast a shadow upon the new marriage and block communication. Adrienne Frydenger, who with her husband, Tom, wrote *The Blended Family,* admitted after the first year of their marriage that she missed her first marriage. She longed for her children to have only one father and one mother, one house with one set of family traditions. She felt like a failure for allowing such upheaval in their lives.

Tom was dismayed at her unhappiness. But because he was a trained counselor, he was able to understand her feelings of grief and loss and to help her come to terms with her confusing emotions. As Adrienne felt free to express her thoughts and Tom was able to listen with objectivity, their good communication was restored.[4]

We who have been divorced have a poor track record. Our desire to counteract our past failure is strong enough to cloud our reason and cause us to have unrealistic expectations for our second marriage. We soon discover that sheer enthusiasm won't guarantee the survival of our new couple relationship.

Even after extensive counseling or, perhaps, a life-changing spiritual experience, we will find ourselves stumbling over our human weakness, responding in old ways to the stressful situations of our post-honeymoon world. We think that this time will be different, but it will be the same in some ways; we think that we know what we are getting into, but we rarely do. In a blending family, the commitment is broader; communication, more hazardous, and compassion, more difficult than in the first marriage. That is reality.

No marital bond is more crucial than that within the blending family. Yet no relationship is more vulnerable to the stress and assault from outside forces. Without a tactical plan for survival, we are in danger of joining the failure statistics for second marriages.

Dealing with the Unexpected

Richard Stuart and Barbara Jacobson (*Second Marriage: Make It Happy! Make It Last!*) speak of "secret contracts" between prospective marriage partners. They recognize

the belief by courting partners that each will continue to act after marriage in accordance with the values and patterns established at the time they agreed to wed. It is understood that the values will prevail throughout their life together, while the daily patterns will continue until circumstances or open discussion necessitate change.[5]

Part of falling in love is discovering that the beloved shares your view of life. Common values are an important basis for a lifetime partnership. But no matter how thoroughly we have explored the issues that will affect our blending family, there are always some that we have left out or skimmed over. There is never enough time during courtship (especially the courtships that we creators of blending families have experienced) to explore every facet of the other's lifestyle and value system.

Phyllis and Don told of their conflict over television.

"It had just never come up before," Phyllis said, "because when Don and I were together before we were married we were either out on a date or at my house *doing* something. We'd fix a meal together or work in the garden or play Monopoly with the kids. When Don wasn't around in the evening or on a Sunday afternoon, I was usually curled up with a good book. Reading has always been one of my greatest pleasures in life. The kids read a lot too, or played in their rooms. We only turned the television on for special programs."

"My love of television came as such a surprise to Phyll," Don cut in. "But watching TV was just something I automatically *did*. When I came home from work at night—to an empty apartment, remember—I switched on the TV before I took my coat off. Then I'd throw something in the microwave and eat while I watched the news and whatever else was on the schedule for the evening. It helped me relax. Besides, the apartment was too quiet without some sound, even if I wasn't paying attention every minute. I really looked forward to the sports events on weekends, and if Phyllis and I couldn't get together they were a compensation. I thought she knew that."

"Of course, I knew that Don watched television more than

I did," Phyllis continued, "but I didn't realize how important it was to him. We'd watched a few things together at my house, like the President's address and the Superbowl—we had his brother over and made a special day of that—but I had no idea he'd be interested in some of the junk that's on every night. Eating in the living room with the umpteenth rerun of some "Mash" episode was my idea of boring. We couldn't carry on a conversation, and if I tried to read I found myself reading the same paragraph over and over."

What Phyllis considered junk was Don's idea of entertainment. It became an issue, and peace was impossible without compromise.

"When we married and Don moved in, we realized how different our established lifestyles were. Poor Don was like a foreigner in an alien land. We sort of divided into opposing camps—my kids and I on one side, smugly superior to the TV addict in our midst, and Don on the other, trying to figure out what his place was in our household."

The actual source of conflict between these two lay in habits they had formed, rather than basic values they both held. Before they married, they'd each developed ways of coping with their singleness. In the stress of adjusting to a new family situation, they clung to old habits as a child does to a tattered security blanket. However, both valued their marital bond above their personal enjoyment of reading or watching television, and it didn't take long for them to develop a lifestyle more beneficial to that bond.

By planning ahead we can avoid some common stumbling blocks. Professionals have identified a number of issues that can create dissension and should be discussed before a second marriage.

Budgeting of income or incomes. Which expenditures are

necessary and which are not? Whose paycheck will pay which bill?

Division of household tasks. Do we think some chores are "women's work" and some reserved for men only? Are we willing to help each other?

Social- and leisure-time activities. Will we continue to go out for dinner once in a while, even when we're no longer dating?

Church attendance. Is there any conflict between our religious backgrounds? Our basic beliefs? Do we both feel the same about making church attendance a part of our lives?

Role of relatives and friends. Are extended family gatherings important to either or both of us? Do we want to keep in contact with old friends? Actively cultivate new ones?

Pursuit of independent interests and hobbies. Will we give each other space to see friends, join a bowling league, take a class?

Continued education and professional development. Is "getting ahead" important to both of us, even if it should mean some sacrifice to family life?

It is easy to minimize some of these issues, expecting them to automatically work out as we go along. We can't preplan everything, and some previously undiscussed matters will "work out," causing hardly a ripple as they arise. But others, such as Phyllis and Don's conflict over their use of leisure time, can weaken the foundation of a new marriage.

Building Unity

In a previous chapter I compared the blending of our family to the building of our prefabricated home. A prefabricated house is one in which many preformed units are brought together to be united upon a common foundation. This approach sounds faster and easier than it actually is. We discovered that a lot of pieces didn't fit very well, and I came to think of our house as a shaky structure, a poor imitation of the real thing. But the ground upon which we built was solid and the foundation was firm. As time went on, our house became a home.

The marital bond is the foundation of the family. It is made up of commitment, communication, and compassion. Our commitment to each other, to the marriage, and to our combined children is like the network of steel that undergirds the concrete base of a house. Our communication is like the concrete slab that overlies the strengthening grid. Compassion—the third dimension—lays the forms of our foundation, containing it within designated boundaries and shaping it for our specific needs and purposes. Compassion sets limits on our communication.

Our husband-wife relationship is paramount in the smooth functioning of our family unit and must rest upon the foundation of commitment and communication, framed by compassion and combined in love. Many times, in a second marriage, we seem to need a kind of superhuman love. The King James Bible has this kind of love in mind when it uses the word "charity." *Zondervan Pictorial Bible Dictionary* gives this definition for charity: "a God-inspired love which includes a respect for and concern for the welfare of the loved one."

Within the blending family, the warmth of the couple relationship is like the open fireplace of a drafty cottage. It draws everyone within the walls to a mutual place of comfort. Our efforts to keep our love covenant glowing are the greatest gifts we can give our family.

Marital bonding is a continual process. There will always be room for refining, redecorating, and remodeling. As we live out our commitment upon a sturdy foundation, there are things we can do to protect our couple-bond.

1. *We can call upon God's love and strength to help us maintain our commitment.* Harry and I pray separately and we

pray together, seeking His will for our lives and for the strength to carry it out. We hold hands at the breakfast table and thank God for what He has given us. Sometimes (not often) we are angry at one another, and we don't feel much like holding hands or even like praying, but we do it.

2. *We can keep our couple relationship as top priority in our blended family.* There are times when life gets very complicated and crisis follows crisis. It's easy to let other things—truly important things—take priority over "us." We try to remember that our couple bond is the cornerstone of our family.

Harry and I went to see some Chinese acrobats at our local theater one night. In one act, two of the performers rode a tandem bicycle around the stage in circles while ten others climbed aboard. Pretty soon the original two were hidden by this mass of grinning acrobats, but the wheels continued to turn, and the apparatus remained upright, because the cyclists kept pedaling together. That's what we need for blending families—for the two on the bottom to keep pedaling together.

3. *We can find and make time for one another.* Early in our marriage, when Harry was going to work early and coming home in the late afternoon, I'd have the coffeepot on when he came in the door and we'd take time then to sit down and share our days with one another. Our coffee hour became a little ritual that we looked forward to. Later, when time and budget allowed, an occasional evening out gave us a chance for some in-depth communication.

4. *We can stay open with one another, having the courage to be vulnerable as we expose our failures and weaknesses.* Pride can get in the way here, but vulnerability is a basic ingredient of intimacy.

When I do something stupid or embarrassing out in the world and can come home and share my foolishness with my husband, it takes the edge off my humiliation. My confession gives Harry the opening to say, "I know just how you feel. Listen to what *I* did yesterday!" If either of us makes a mistake on the checkbook or backs the car into the mailbox, we don't have to "cover up" or weave any tangled webs of deceit.

5. *We can try to communicate our love in words, actions, and attitudes.* The more we learn about each other, the more opportunity we have to act out our love in little ways. We begin to know which of our words bring comfort and encouragement and which will irritate or anger. As we expose our own Achilles' heels to each other, we trust each other to be considerate of these sensitive areas.

6. *We who have been forgiven so much by God can be willing to forgive each other for all the times we fail to do any of the above!*

Harry and I adopted those as our ground rules and framed them with good intentions. We haven't always followed them, especially in the beginning, before we knew God in a personal way. But we have stumbled along, sustained by His grace, led by His guidance when we could understand it. Gradually—sometimes painfully—we've achieved a relationship that serves us well.

To quote Dwight Small, "In every marriage the inherent dangers are great and the privileges colossal. The gamble is for keeps. Imagine the miracle of it. . . ."[6]

6
Other People's Children

I had no problem with the idea of taking on Jean's son," one disillusioned stepfather admitted. "I really looked forward to his living with us and to being a father to him—but within a week there was trouble. I resented his attitude toward me so much that it swallowed up every good intention. He deliberately ignored me when I spoke to him—even if all I said was 'good morning, Ryan' or 'how did school go today?' If he had something to say to his mother, he turned his back on me and whispered so I couldn't overhear. Jean felt terrible about it, too, but she couldn't seem to do anything about it. I was furious with him for making us both suffer. Our pastor reminded me that love is really a decision and that I didn't have to 'feel' anything. So I gritted my teeth and decided to keep trying. In the long run it was worth it, but it was pretty hard on the marriage for awhile."

Although the couple relationship has top priority in the blending family, it does not exist in a vacuum. It is intertwined with and stressed by the other relationships within the family, especially between stepparent and stepchild.

Many of us—perhaps the majority of us—begin our stepparenting with enthusiasm. The prospect of helping a child to grow into a happy, well-adjusted adult is exciting and challenging. If the child has been deprived of one of his parents by death or desertion, our role will be that of full-time parent and we can be assured that we are needed. If our spouse will have part-time custody of his child, we look forward to supporting him in his role. In parenting our stepchild, we have the opportunity to manifest our love and commitment to our partner.

Our enthusiasm, however, can quickly turn to bewilderment if our first efforts are met with rejection. The stepchild comes to the remarriage wounded by what has happened in his life, defensive against further hurt, and often behaving badly. We must realize that he is still working through the pain of his loss and that his behavior may be rooted in that pain. His "acting out" can confound the most well-intentioned stepparent. Enough conflict between stepparent and stepchild may erode the developing couple relationship beyond repair.

No matter how committed, compassionate, and skilled in communication we are with one another, our marital bond cannot compete with the parent-child bond that each of us brings to the marriage. Competition is not the issue. For the harmonious blending of persons, there can be no competition, only complement, where relationships combine to complete that which was incomplete.

"All You Have to Do Is Love Them"?

Experts say that the proving time for step relationships takes two to five years. Within that time, they say, the blending family will either split or strengthen.

When Harry and I began to talk about combining our large families, I sought the guidance of a counselor. He helped me to explore the many problems inherent in our situation, leaving me with these memorable and profound words, "All you really have to do is love them.'' I came away reassured, confident that I could easily fulfill that requirement.

I loved all children, I thought, having had unlimited experience with my own and with other little people of our neighborhood. Therefore, I couldn't believe the hatred that filled my soul the first time one of Harry's unruly children was mean to one of my little angels. Like a mother bear, I struck out in defense of my own. Only later could I see the hardness of my unreliable heart.

During the first days of our family merger, I found that love for my husband's children did not happen automatically. My human love was a fragile, puny thing. It wilted at the disdain of a ten-year-old child who looked at my meat loaf as if something had died on his plate. It faded at the rebuff of a six-year-old, who resisted my efforts to wipe away his tears after a tumble from his bike.

I looked at these five youngsters—children who were the result of a long-ago love between Harry and another woman— and knew that I had overestimated my capacity to love them. Fortunately, God was waiting in the wings for my cry of despair.

In the first weeks of my own blending family I came to understand that the love I needed for Harry's children (and the respect I desired from them) needed time to grow. To expect instant affection and harmony between our diverse personalities was unrealistic—one more idealistic dream to be shelved in favor of reality.

Blood relationships are different from all others in that they start ''from scratch.'' Emotional bonding usually takes place quickly. Nonblood relationships have an element of choice and are apt to fail if they are forced. Good ones develop slowly and may be counted among the treasures of a lifetime. For stronger bonds often exist between partners in happy marriages or in deep, abiding friendships than between individuals who happen to share a common ancestry.

Relationships and love grow, even between those with close blood ties, over time. But what does a new stepparent do in the meantime, as the words "All you have to do is love them" reverberate in her aching head? The answer to that comes with the understanding of what love is.

Charles Swindoll summarized the characteristics of love identified in 1 Corinthians 13:4–7 in five statements, which he calls the ABC's of love:

1. I **accept** you as you are.
2. I **believe** you are valuable.
3. I **care** when you hurt.
4. I **desire** only what is best for you.
5. I **erase** all offenses.[1]

I would suggest the addition of three R's:

1. Realize that instant love is a myth and that bonding is a process.
2. Reaffirm your commitment to the children you have chosen to raise and to the parent who trusts you with their care.
3. Resolve to act out your love with understanding and compassion.

One young woman rebelled at such a selfless stance. "I tried so hard with my husband's fourteen-year-old daughter— thought we'd be friends from the beginning, as she seemed to accept me when her dad and I were going together. But after we were married, nothing I did was right. She made fun of my clothes, ridiculed my friends, and barely tolerated my cooking. I wasn't mature enough myself to understand where she was coming from, and I got right down on her level. If she rejected me, then forget it—I'd just quit trying. Rather than set myself up for more hurt, I acted like she didn't exist.

"My older sister came to dinner one night and read me the riot act. She said I was 'psychologically abusing' her—that that was just as bad as physical abuse. Deep down I knew that I had been acting like an adolescent myself. I went to talk to our pastor, and he called my stepdaughter in, and we both cried. It didn't solve all our problems right away, but I did try harder. Once in awhile I'd do some little thing for her, like bringing in a tray of hot chocolate and popcorn when her friends were over, and she'd be surprised and appreciative. The better we got along, the happier her father was, of course."

Every relationship within the blended family affects every other. The same principles apply to the building and maintenance of the stepparent/stepchild relationship as to that between spouses: commitment, communication, and compassion offered in love, freely and without expectation of return. That is a big order for a person struggling with his own problems of adjustment. It takes charity—agape love. We must constantly call upon the love of God for us and through us if we are to survive the blending process.

Harry and I look back in amazement at our own ignorance. "I was so naive," he said. "I never thought about the fact that each of us had to relate to ten other people. I thought when we got together that everyone would just fall into line and get along. We were fortunate that they got along as well as they did."

In her book *Changepoints,* Joyce Landorf says that a child between five and twelve is in the gullible years—he believes everything he hears, particularly from parents, family and teachers. At this stage of life, she tells us, we can program them like little computers—for better or for worse—simply by our words and actions.[2]

All of our children's ages fell within that span when our

prefamily interaction began. Perhaps their malleable ages helped to promote their cooperation. Had I understood the power of our words to shape character and personality, I might have been afraid to speak at all. Had I realized then our tremendous responsibility in "programming" our youngsters, I might have turned and run away.

"Who's in Charge Here?"

The question of a stepparent's authority is a source of conflict in nearly every blending family. Many remarrying men and women are glad to share the burden of child rearing with their spouse, but there are those who hold back in misdirected fear for their child's welfare.

"Frank knew absolutely nothing about girls when we got married," said Sally. "He had one son and two brothers—hadn't even had a sister or close girl cousins. I just couldn't stay out of his attempts to discipline my girls, even though he was always fair enough. Actually, the girls were hungry for a man's guidance, and Frank had established enough rapport with them that they could accept him in a father role. I was the one who had the problem with it."

For me it was a matter of trust. I wouldn't have wanted to entrust my children's future welfare to another adult whose integrity was in question or whose values were significantly different from my own. I wouldn't have been willing to share my parenting with such a man, nor would I have wanted him anywhere within my children's sphere of influence.

Harry and I had become friends before we fell in love, and we'd spent a lot of time in deep conversation, sharing our ideas and dreams with one another. By the time we'd decided to marry, I knew what kind of person he was. I had come to admire his honesty, his patience, and his kindness, and I respected his determination to reunite his scattered family. Because of what I knew of his character, I was willing to trust him in a position of authority over my children, theoretically speaking. In actual practice it was a different matter.

One of the first times that Harry used his authority to admonish one of my youngsters is indelibly inscribed in my memory. One evening nine-year-old Tom turned on the water for his bath, added a generous dollop of bubble liquid, and wandered off to inspect some treasure he'd brought home in the pocket of his jeans. I was puttering in the kitchen when I heard the unfamiliar sound of a large hand meeting a small bottom. Within seconds I was at my son's side, glaring incredulously at my husband.

"Well, look at that tub!" he exclaimed, needlessly pointing at a layer of foam that all but obscured the fixture in question.

"I was just *going* to turn it off, Mom," protested Tommy, wide-eyed with amazement at this sharp reaction from his gentle stepfather.

"You spanked him for *that*?" I asked, unable to comprehend such behavior from my trusted spouse.

"You could hardly call one little swat a spanking," Harry answered, looking from me to Tom for some kind of understanding. "What am I supposed to do, just stand there and watch him waste water?"

That, of course, was the crux of the problem. In our former household, my children and I enjoyed the unlimited use of warm water in our baths and showers, without a thought for conservation of this abundant commodity. The conservation of water and heat was a major issue to Harry, an insignificant matter to me. It was one of the many minor values upon which we differed. The subject had never come up for discussion before the tub incident.

Harry was right in placing importance on the saving of hot water, and I had no reasonable argument, but the emotional impact of seeing (or hearing) another adult strike my child was unsettling. I'd been willing, I thought, to share my parental role with my husband, but at the first gentle swat (and probably the last) I found myself ready to do battle.

Although the role of authority should be approached with caution and sensitivity, it is an appropriate one for the stepparent of young children. God's plan for family involves two parents in complementary positions. To be a parent to a stepchild is to accept responsibility for his care and guidance.

There is a paradox in the fact that the strength of the couple relationship determines whether or not the family will function successfully. In a blended family, that relationship is constantly under pressure from the large and small issues involving the children. To put it another way, the survival of the blended family is crucial to the welfare of our displaced children; yet it is the care and discipline of these children that become the center of conflict in most remarriages. Like the chicken and the egg, the success of one both follows and precedes the success of the other.

We can't parent our stepchildren without their permission. No discipline will work unless the child is basically willing to obey parental authority. When children are young we can wield the power of our adult position in the family, but our influence for good will be temporary at best.

There is a significant difference between the building of a relationship between stepparent and stepchild and the building of the couple relationship. The improvement of the marital bond is valued and sought after by both partners. In forming ties with our stepchildren, it is often a one-way street, with the child indifferent or actively resistant and the stepparent making the only effort. It is not easy for a stepparent who is fighting his own battle with insecurity and is met with rejection at every well-intentioned turn. It can be warfare, and we don't go to war unarmed.

Our first need is to recognize our limitations. We have missed the bonding stage that the natural parent takes for granted. It is the foundation for his ability to discipline. A natural parent's goal is not that his child should love him above all, but that his child will submit to his guidance and discipline. Discipline is teaching, and what we are about, or "our goal as parents," is the teaching of our children to become independent, productive and *self*-disciplined adults.

The biological parent spends the first months of her child's life forming a love bond with that child as she responds to the infant's needs. By the time discipline is in order, the child is malleable and trusting—willing to respond to this source of all love and comfort. However, stepparents lack such bonding. We can't start in the middle with the disciplinary phase until we have built a bridge of rapport or mutual trust and understanding. Love may not come easily, but a friendly relationship between stepparent and stepchild is a good beginning.

Are We Building Roadblocks or Bridges?

A child brings a lot of emotional baggage to his restructured family. This is one of many roadblocks to relationship building with his stepparent. His security is shaken by the drastic changes in his life. Conflicting loyalties to his natural parents (whether death or divorce has separated them) hurt and confuse him, and disappointment and disillusionment cause him to erect barriers of defense against further pain. In the case of divorce, he rarely understands what *really* happened to *his* mom and dad and suspects he may be responsible in some way.

Until we can put our own sensitivity aside and muster the compassion necessary to build a bridge at this child's point of need, we can make little progress toward a satisfactory relationship. As we build bridges and help our children to connect with us, their defenses will come down and bonding can begin.

Children will test us with rejection, defiance, and manipulation. Human love will have difficulty withstanding the test. To love the unlovable is possible only when we can become a channel for God's unconditional love. That requires patience, persistence, and—above all—prayer.

Charlotte, stepmother of three lively boys, shared her experience. "Guy's sons were really impossible. They resented me and they let me know it. I felt guilty, because I'd meant to love them, and I couldn't seem to get past my anger at them. I prayed about it, but I told myself that God understood and probably didn't expect any more of me. One day I had the definite impression that He said, 'I love them, Charlotte.' Of course He did! He made them, and they were precious to Him. I knew He loved me too, and maybe—if I'd let Him—He could use me to express His love to those little boys. Oh, it didn't happen overnight, believe me. But in spite of myself, I began to look at them with different eyes. I began to feel a real fondness for them, and of course they responded. Actually, it was because I loved Guy so much that I didn't want to see him hurt by my unloving attitude toward his kids."

Adolescent children of the same sex as the stepparent present the greatest problem in family blending, with the relationship between stepmother and stepdaughter the most difficult. They are apt to find themselves in tense competition for the attention of the man they both love. Time may mellow the relationship, but it is usually strained in the beginning.

My experience with Harry's daughter was a contradiction. If one single factor tipped the scales in favor of harmony within our family, it was Joan's willingness to accept me as her mother and her stepsiblings as her own. I needed help desperately, and I called upon our two older girls for their hands in the kitchen and their help with the cleaning. This created a closeness between the stepsisters, Laurie and Joan, and a camaraderie among the three of us that brightened all the years of our family blending. Even today, Joan and Laurie are as close as most "blood" sisters.

My bridge-building with the boys was not so easy. If they didn't warm to my advances immediately, hurt pride caused me to back off. I wanted them to like and understand me, but Harry's younger boys were not ready to bond with another mother-figure, and the older ones lived in some preadolescent masculine realm beyond my understanding. Unlike their sister, they could find little basis for communication with me.

Often, if we can understand the feelings of children caught up in the shuffle of remarriage we have a basis for beginning to build relationships. Beyond the crucial area of new relationships are many more adjustments that may be facing them. Here are only a few:

1. A new place to call home, or an old one reorganized
2. A change in schools
3. An unfamiliar neighborhood
4. Sharing a bedroom or losing privacy
5. New rules and patterns of discipline
6. Unfamiliar holiday rituals, loss of cherished tradition
7. Changed socioeconomic status.

In each of these areas there is a loss of the familiar and the stress of trying to adapt to the unfamiliar. A child may feel resentment and anger over his inability to control his circumstances. He mourns the loss of his own room, his friends, the old neighborhood, his Scout leader; he is confused over where he fits in the reconstructed family and what is expected of him. Often he has retained the fantasy of his natural parents reuniting, and the remarriage puts to death that dream.

Conflicting loyalties make bonding with the new stepparent difficult. He doesn't want to risk losing another parent, so he refuses to accept the stepparent in that role. He may actually resist any tendency to like his stepparent, because in doing so he would lose a convenient target for his anger or feel like a traitor to his natural parent. He will suffer from jealousy of new family members who come between him and his natural parent and of stepsiblings who appear to have more privileges.

The relationship between the child and his natural parent is subject to change as the parent moves from a single state to a new marriage. A single parent and his or her child often become increasingly interdependent after a broken marriage. This relationship will relax gradually as child and parent find renewed security in a two-parent household, but that sense of security may be slow in developing. In the meantime, patience is required of parent and stepparent alike.

Rachel and her twelve-year-old daughter, Deanna, had shared every confidence during the two years after Rachel's husband, Tony, died.

"It was wonderful closeness," Rachel recalled. "We helped each other through the grieving time. When Chet came into our lives, Deanna was as excited as I was. We included her in most of our activities. Chet was always willing to take Dee and her friends roller skating or to the beach or anywhere they wanted to go. We found time for ourselves when Dee was in school or away for an evening.

"But after we were married, she thought our threesome should continue. If we closed our bedroom door, she pouted, and when Chet's boys came for the summer, she was downright disagreeable. She began to hint that I was being disloyal to her father's memory."

"I didn't know much about adolescent girls," Chet interjected, "but I remembered my sisters talking about their daughters and how temperamental they could be at that stage. Deanna and I had begun a pretty good relationship before Rachel and I were married, so I thought it would work out eventually. I had a problem with her attitude toward my boys though. I'd taken it for granted that she'd like them."

Chet was right about things working out. When Deanna realized that he didn't stop loving her when his sons came and that her mother still needed her special feminine companionship, she began to look forward to their arrival. When Rachel made an effort to plan family activities especially suitable for the boys, Deanna joined in with her own ideas for their pleasure.

"Dee and I had gotten to be more like chums than like mother and daughter, and it was hard for her when Chet became my primary relationship. But she was getting to the age when kids start being independent anyway, so she relaxed her grip on me sort of naturally."

Some Roadblocks Are Already in Place

Relationships within our blending family were far more complex than in the average stepfamily. Harry had not lived with his children for a number of years. His five children had been in three separate foster homes and had seen each other only sporadically. Aside from their traumatic separation from their familiar settings—difficult in spite of the fact that it was a move toward the "normalizing" of their lives—they had the stress of adjusting to nearly every other individual in our blending family.

Harry Jr. suffered from severe asthma, aggravated by the emotional strain of moving from a position of an only child in his foster family to the middle one of nine in our combination family. Steve, the oldest, was subject to seizures and developmentally disabled (a fact that became clear only gradually after months and years of struggling to cope with his erratic and inappropriate behavior). Six-year-old Mark silently mourned his foster family, the only family he could remember; his eight-year-old brother, Greg, hid his own burden of pain behind a facade of phony cheerfulness.

On their first day of school in our new community, Harry Jr. stayed home with a frightening attack of asthma, and Steve had a seizure on the playground. The two boys and I spent the afternoon at the local medical clinic, while the remaining seven came home on the bus to an empty house.

I'd had visions of standing on the doorstep with open arms as I welcomed them back to the nest. The scent of freshly baked cookies would beckon them inside, and—over a pitcher of lemonade—I'd listen with rapt attention as they eagerly shared their "first day" adventures. Instead, I was trapped by the unexpected—a harbinger of days to come. Time after time my idealistic intentions crumbled in the face of stark reality. I was committed to caring for the physical needs of my stepchildren, and there never seemed to be enough time left over for developing relationships. We did, eventually, build our bridges of rapport, but it was slow going.

Stepchildren often are the innocent victims of a parent's frustration and resentment—frustration over the inability to meet everyone's needs and resentment that time spent on stepchildren is taken from one's natural children. This, I've found, is a common feeling among stepmothers. We are often guilty over our failure to equalize affection between stepchildren and natural children—an unnecessary burden, the professionals say. Each child in the blending family deserves our consideration and respect. To try to force more than that is to invite disappointment.

Children of blending families may be embarrassed by the

fact that their family structures are "different." In a small town a child may hear something like this: "So your name's Barton? Is your dad Sam Barton, down at the feed mill? Or are you from the Bartons over on Cider Mill Drive? I'll bet I know your older brother." Such questions may be awkward for a child adjusting to living with a family name different from his own surname. He's embarrassed to explain that his dad lives in Middleton, Iowa, along with his only brother, who decided to stay with his father when his mother married Tom Smith.

We need to help our children find acceptable outlets for the feelings of anger, confusion, or fear that are almost certain by-products of the remarriage shuffle. If a child is forced to turn his pain inward, he may withdraw from the very relationships that can help him most. He may become excessively moody or irritable or aggressive. His schoolwork may suffer as he loses motivation and concentration.

If we see these symptoms of distress in our own children, we will likely respond with sympathy (mixed, perhaps, with guilt). When our stepchildren are moody, angry, or unmotivated in school, we are quick to label them as uncooperative or "hard to get along with."

"Jason is a very difficult child," declared his stepmother in a group discussion. "He is openly defiant whenever I ask him to do anything, and he spends a lot of time in his room, just lying on his bed and staring at the ceiling. Jim assures me that he's been a good student, but I haven't seen much evidence of it. He's continually late with his assignments, and he doesn't seem to care."

"How about Craig, your own boy?" someone asked. "Is he adjusting well to your remarriage?"

"Oh, poor little Craig," his mother answered. "He looks so sad sometimes, it breaks my heart. Jim gets impatient with him—says he mopes around too much—but I can see what he's going through."

That conversation graphically demonstrates a contrast in perspectives.

"I felt emotionally wrung out after the first six months with my stepdaughter," said Paula. "At fifteen she was in the throes of adolescent rebellion. My friends assured me that I could be going through the same kind of thing with a daughter of my own, if I had one. But that's one of the problems—with someone else's kids you don't start at the beginning. I knew that if I'd been around when Amy was growing up I'd have understood her better. My own feelings of insecurity got in the way. This kid could really hurt my feelings without half trying. I don't think we would have made it without counseling. And if Amy and I had kept on battling, my marriage to her father would have been on the line. We're really good friends now, and it was worth the hassle."

The bottom line is this: each child is unique—a very special combination of genes and personality traits, with his own set of hopes and fears and experiences. We must discover the roadblocks that stand in the way of his becoming secure and happy within our blended family. We must learn to look beneath his surface behavior and bring comfort to his wounds.

Reaching Out

But how do we reach a child who has erected barriers or roadblocks against us? We begin with love—that agape kind of love that is a deliberate choice, rather than an emotional response. Only with love can we begin to provide him with a safe and secure place in which to grow up, a place where he is free to be himself. He needs space of his own; a feeling of belonging to and with the significant people in his life; acceptance of his awkwardness and forgiveness for his mistakes; open communication, where he can freely express his thoughts without censure—a two-way bridge, where his parents take the lead by being open and honest with their own thoughts and feelings.

So far in this book we've talked about commitment, communication, compassion, and charity. At this point we can add another "c" word to that list: courage. When we feel rejected by our stepchildren, it is hard to make ourselves more vulnerable by revealing our own weaknesses. Our natural inclination is to withdraw behind a fortress of pride rather than subject our tender psyches to further rebuff. But the opportunity for a close bond with our stepchild is worth the risk of occasional hurt feelings.

When we remember that God Himself came down to our human level to communicate with us, can we do less than swallow a little pride to bridge the gap of years with our children? More often than not, our own straightforwardness will be met with a willingness to understand and reciprocate in kind. To confide in a child is to say, "I trust you enough to share these feelings with you, and I care what you think of me."

Some discretion should be used here, of course. Our children do not need to be burdened with confidences beyond their understanding. A stepchild does not need to hear that his father has turned out to be a miserable disappointment as a husband, and our biological child should not be asked to sympathize with us over the sins of his absent parent.

In reaching out to draw our children into a relationship within the new family circle, we can create opportunities for working together toward some mutual goal. Planting a vegetable garden, building a doghouse, or painting *his* room—important tasks within the range of his abilities will not only help him achieve a sense of competence but will instill in him a sense of belonging. Our children need encouragement and appreciation if they are to develop a feeling of self-worth.

Paul gives us specific instructions for encouraging one another in Philippians 4:8:

> Finally, brothers, whatever is true, whatever is noble, whatever is right, whatever is pure, whatever is lovely, whatever is admirable—if anything is excellent or praiseworthy—think about such things.

Most of us can remember the words of a parent or teacher who made us feel worthy and, perhaps, changed the course of our lives. I am a writer today because a fifth-grade teacher wrote on a report, "Good! You have a real talent for writing, Carolyn."

Another way to draw closer to our stepchildren is to show interest in whatever absorbs their attention. Maybe you recoil at the loud rock music your teenager loves, but you can suppress your distaste and ask a few questions. He'll probably be surprised and pleased at your interest.

"Verne's two boys were really into high school football," said Leona, as we talked about sharing interests. "For awhile I went along to the Friday night games, just so I wouldn't have to sit home alone, but my lack of enthusiasm showed. One day I saw something about football team formations on the back of a cereal box, written so simply that even I could understand it. That sent me to the encyclopedia for a little more basic information.

"The guys had been in the habit of discussing the games over my head, and the first time I joined in with an intelligent comment they were amazed. Todd and James looked at me with new respect then—even addressed me directly once in awhile, so I had to keep up my efforts to understand what was going on.

I began to really enjoy the games, and it made a difference in my relationship with my stepsons.''

The one-to-one moments spent alone with a child are the building blocks of the bond that we hope to establish. As father and stepson wash the family car together, the boy finds opportunity to share his dream of someday having a car of his own. As mother and stepdaughter spend an afternoon sewing a new dress for the high school prom, there is space for intimate conversation about boys and dating and sexuality—subjects that don't come easily in the everyday whirl of family activity.

Most of us have an easier time expressing our deeper thoughts on a one-to-one basis, and it is these special times when bridges of communication are reinforced and parent-child bonds are strengthened. Sometimes a stepparent can find a special and unique area of communication with his stepchild, a point of contact with him alone. Although Harry Jr. and I clashed frequently during his growing-up years, we had one such point of contact. He suffered from asthma, and so did I. Even when I was annoyed with him for bringing on a wheezing attack by his own antics, I knew how it felt to struggle for breath, and he knew I knew it. Years later I found a tiny, ancient school picture of myself that had somehow fallen into his hands. On the back he'd written the words, "Mom—had asthma." He'd found a point of contact with me.

Marian tried many things with her stepdaughter before she hit upon a mutual interest. "I loved knitting and crocheting and all kinds of needlework," she said, "and I tried to get Melissa started with some project, but she just wasn't interested. She loved horses and she had riding companions her own age. I'd never been around animals and I was half afraid of them, so we couldn't find any common ground there.

"One rainy day she picked up my old copy of *Anne of Green Gables,* which I'd loved as a child her age, and asked if she could read it. She was enchanted! I dug out the rest of the series and started rereading it myself. The thing was that we'd finally found something to talk about. When the film series came on public television, we watched it together. Somehow, the fact that we both loved the same stories meant that we felt the same way about important things. It created a closeness between us that we hadn't been able to achieve before."

Marian's efforts to find a bridge of communication with Melissa were rewarded, and the entire family unit benefited from their tighter bond. It doesn't always happen, but if we look hard enough we can usually find an area of mutuality.

One adult friend told me about her experience with her stepmother, a cold, proud woman who had married her father without making any commitment to his teenaged daughter.

"We were like two ships that passed in the night," my friend said. "Each of us had our own separate relationship with my dad, but none with each other. Then Grace, my stepmother, developed a painful sciatic condition and had to have ice packs and massage three times a day. Guess who got that job when my dad was at work!

"In the beginning we both hated it. She resented being dependent on me, and I resented performing this intimate service for her. But neither of us was made of steel. I could see her misery, and when my massaging her back and leg relieved her pain, I felt good about helping. And she couldn't help but respond to me and my efforts. She'd say things like, 'I know you'd rather be doing something with your friends. Sorry to be such a burden.' The more she appreciated me, the better I felt toward her.

"We never got really close—I went away to school soon after that and never lived at home again, but we'd shared something special, and I don't think either of us ever forgot it."

Communicating without Words

Communication within the family extends far beyond the spoken words. We send messages by eye contact, or lack of it; touch, or avoidance of it; a small act of consideration, or the omission of it.

Johnny leaps from the steps of the school bus, prances down the driveway, and bursts through the door, calling "I'm home!" His mother greets him with a smile and a hug, brings out a snack of milk and cookies, and sits down at the table with him to ask about his day. Only a few words pass between them, but they are communicating love and delight in being together again.

Moments like these are the ones that emit a warm glow when called up from our memory file years later. We may forget the details, but somewhere along the way our minds have made a connection between "home" and "love."

Johnny's friend, Charles, gets off the bus at the next stop. He wanders across his front yard, kicking at pebbles and detouring through a couple of mud puddles as he fishes for the house key pinned inside his jeans' pocket. Inside the empty house, a note on the kitchen table reminds him to change his clothes and feed "that pesky dog."

The contrast is obvious and perhaps oversimplified. Most children experience a combination of both kinds of receptions in their growing-up years. Most parents try to balance the account in favor of "cookie days." As stepparents, we try all the harder.

A touch of the hand, a pat on the shoulder, a look of compassion across the room to a child struggling with a difficult homework assignment—these are silent messages that communicate our love and concern.

Mark, Harry's youngest boy, came home from Cub Scout meeting one afternoon to announce that "our leader, Mrs. Moniot, hugged me for *no reason*!" Hugs for "no reason" go a long way toward building a child's self-esteem. They say, "I appreciate you, just because you're you."

We provide mirrors in which our children can see the reflections of who they are. If we smile and coo at an infant and call him "precious," he doesn't know what the word means. But he smiles and coos back because we have made him feel good. He senses his own value. The message he has received is, "You're something special."

In his book *How To Really Love Your Child,* Dr. Ross Campbell says that every child is continually asking, "Do you love me?"—if not verbally, by his behavior.[3] Over the past generations we have become increasingly aware of the emotional and psychological needs of our children. We hear the cry in the poignant message of a six-year-old's scrawl on a homemade card—"I love you. Do you love me?" We see, if we look with compassionate eyes, the underlying hurt in the belligerence of the adolescent or the withdrawal of the teenager.

Looking back on our own family, I can see the many ways in which each child sought affirmation of his or her specialness. I know now that a child's sense of his own value develops bit by bit as he takes in and registers the responses of those around him. He has a deep, throbbing need for affection, acceptance, and approval—a need parallel to that of his physical need for food. How we as stepparents respond to that need will have a significant effect on the rest of his life.

Dennis Guernsey says, "All that we really know about ourselves as people is what we've experienced in the responses of others to us, especially in the 'significant others.'[4] And what we know about ourselves is the foundation for our self-esteem, or lack of it."

We stepparents become "significant others" to children whose self-concept has already been shaped by the experiences and persons of his earlier years. But that is not the final picture.

Research now shows that a child's personality is not set in cement by age 5 or 6. Stepparents can have a profound influence upon a child of any age. People are changed by love.

We can and will make a difference in the lives of "other people's children." Whether that difference is positive or negative will be determined by how well we are able to connect with them and how they will see themselves through our eyes.

7
Unexpected Adjustments

When we begin to take inventory of everyone who is going to have to be blended into a family, we may have a lot more to cope with than we anticipated. We had expected to be able to concentrate on the crucial relationships with our new spouses and their children, but we may find ourselves in a tangle of complex relationships. Consider the following combinations:

1. Two sets of children sharing one home and one set of parents.

2. The children of one spouse interacting periodically with their stepparent's noncustodial children.

3. One or two sets of children joined by a new addition to the family.

4. A newly formed family where a live-in grandparent continues to be a significant member.

Within each of these configurations are endless combinations of ages, temperaments, and special problems. Here is just one unique situation as described by Ellie, mother of a handicapped daughter.

"Pam's brothers had been around her forever and had long ago learned to love and accept her. When Scooter, Gary's son, came into our family, he was obviously embarrassed and uncomfortable around Pam. He solved his problem with her by avoiding any contact with her—something my boys couldn't understand. We had set up a system within our family—our family before Gary and I were married—that revolved around and protected Pam. I couldn't have changed that and didn't want to. Gary cooperated as much as he could, and Scooter chose to function outside of our system."

Sibling Rivalry

Sibling rivalry began with the first family and resulted in murder between brothers (Gen. 4:8). The incidence of stepsibling conflict escalates with the number of combination families formed every day. Our task is to keep discordance of our combined children at a minimum and to promote harmonious relationships between all the diverse personalities of our blending families.

Our own family was atypical because Harry's children had been separated from one another and from him for several years. In our restructured family, they had not only the task of adjustment to stepsiblings but to one another. My children, on the other hand, were suddenly outnumbered by the sudden influx of five full-time stepsiblings who threatened to swallow up much of their mother's time and attention. In-house sibling rivalry must have been in full swing, but Harry and I were too busy to notice.

Children can be helped, but not forced, into harmonious relationships with each other. Their first basis for relationship is the sharing of membership within a unique group of people. Fairness demands that members have equally important places within the family. Stepsiblings lack the blood relationship and common "history," but their lives have been brought together (as are those of natural children) by two parents who love each other. They are related first, not by blood connection, but by the bond between two people committed to their care. From that foundation, the gap in blood-relatedness of the stepsiblings will be bridged and diminished according to the things they find to share as the family blends.

Sometimes the gap is too wide to bridge because of age, personality, or temperament difference. Other times the sharing of the parent/stepparent is more divisive than uniting. A child who is insecure in his relationship with his natural parent may feel a real loss at the intrusion of a stepparent and his children, who steal the precious crumbs of his mother's attention from him.

The roots of sibling rivalry originate in the soil of human selfishness. Every child is reluctant to share his parent with another. It is natural for him to rebel in the beginning—whether it is in response to a new baby in the family or a new stepsibling. As he grows older he will see the logic in congenial brotherhood and reap some of its benefits, but rivalry with his siblings will continue to exist in some form.

There are three things that we as parents can do to help our children and stepchildren live in harmony together.

1. We can relate to each child as an individual, valued within the family for who he is and for his unique contribution to the family.

2. We can be united in our agreement about methods of discipline and expectations for behavior. On that basis, we can be scrupulously fair in applying discipline and extending privileges.

3. We can provide ways for everyone to work and play together.

As we continue to strengthen our bonds with our spouse's children, we should constantly reassure our own children of our unwavering love and loyalty. In the beginning of the blending family, one-to-one times are especially crucial for the blood-related parent and child. These special times will reassure him of the continuing relationship with his natural parent and take the edge off his resentment of stepsiblings who now share his parent's attention.

One mother confessed that she had gone to extremes in that direction.

"I bent over backwards to assure Courtney that things hadn't changed between us—even made the mistake of tempering my affectionate overtures to my stepchildren, thinking that would keep Courtney from feeling jealous or insecure. The trouble was that she followed my lead and treated Herb's girls with kind of courteous indifference—like temporary houseguests. As I got closer to my stepdaughters, Courtney loosened up, too, and began treating them more like family."

As a child feels secure in the acceptance and appreciation shown for him by his parent and stepparent, he will find less reason for jealousy of his stepsiblings. But don't be dismayed if it doesn't disappear altogether. Dr. James Dobson has this to say about sibling rivalry:

> Conflict between siblings is as natural as eating and sleeping. In fact, it could almost be considered unnatural for them to coexist in constant harmony, although that does occur occasionally.[1]

His advice for parents is to set up a balance of power between siblings by establishing some rules to lessen the conflict. This is particularly important in a blending family. Parent and stepparent must be united in the efforts to set guidelines and limits for all children involved.

In his lecture series, "Turn Your Heart Toward Home," Dr. Dobson explains that children want limits for their behavior. His illustration describes what happened when a chain link fence was removed from around a school playground. The idea was to give the children more of a sense of space and freedom, but it had the opposite effect. The children moved in from the perimeters, away from the former boundaries, to cluster together toward the center of the playground. Rather than inhibiting them, the fence had given them a feeling of security and safety.

Equalizing limits and privileges will promote harmony within the blending family. When two sets of children who have experienced different patterns of discipline move in together—or are brought together frequently—chaos will reign unless a new family system is established. Within that system, the parent and stepparent will share authority over their combined children. (Here is a place where I believe a stepfather should move very slowly in assuming his biblical role of authority over the family.)

For the children to cooperate with the parents and with each other, they must perceive their leaders to be fair and just. When old rules are adjusted or new rules established, the children must be helped to understand that the change is not just the whim of their stepparents, but an innovation to benefit the whole family.

Open discussions at a family council are a good idea. With parents retaining their rightful leadership roles, the children can help establish some basic "house rules." Here every family member is encouraged to express his ideas and air his grievances. The guidelines for a family council are simple: Everyone has the right to speak and everyone has the obligation to listen. If children are invited to express themselves in this kind of atmosphere, the build-up of resentment toward parent, sibling, or stepsibling can be minimized.

The council may come together at regular, predetermined

intervals when everyone can be expected to be at home, or it may be an informal gathering as the opportunity arises.

Our best family discussions happened at the dinner table, when our evening meal brought us together at the end of the day. Our gatherings had no formal structure, but the opportunity was there for the exchange of ideas and complaints. I'm not sure that everyone had an equal voice or the courtesy of anyone's undivided attention—the older kids probably drowned out the younger ones—but it was the closest we came to a family council.

Dobson suggests that the less significant conflicts between siblings be ignored, allowing the youngsters to fight their own battles. This (believe me!) is more difficult in a blending family than in a nuclear one. Scuffles and bickering between natural siblings are usually accepted by the parent as a normal part of the family life. It is harder in a blending family for the biological parent to withdraw from the center of conflict between her own child and his stepsibling.

"That was a hard thing for me in my new marriage," said Edith, mother of two and stepmother of three. "I had forced my rather placid and cheerful kids into a situation where they were continually subjected to the teasing and sarcasm of Walter's boys, and I felt they deserved my protection. I was always jumping into the middle of every little scrap, which only created more resentment on both sides. Not to mention the resentment I felt for Walt because he didn't do something about his rowdy sons.

"Finally, a friend pointed out to me that I didn't feel it necessary to get involved in every squabble between my kids and their playmates in the neighborhood, and maybe I could try looking at Walt's kids more objectively. The more I stayed out of it, the better they got along. His weren't really mean kids—just boisterous. We did make some rules about invading each other's privacy and saying cruel things to one another.''

Privileges will vary with differences in age and demonstrations of maturity, but they should be impartially extended to both sets of children. The important thing is for children to perceive that their parents are making every effort to be fair.

As we have seen, the emotional basis of sibling rivalry is a child's unwillingness to share his parents. We can abort the damaging effects of such rivalry by gratifying his desire for our time and attention. We can have unique, one-to-one relationships with each child, building such ties slowly with our stepchildren and maintaining those preexistent ones with our own children.

Older Children

In many blending families, some or all of one or both sets of children will have grown and left home before the remarriage. Because the role of parenting continues for a lifetime, we are right in desiring and working toward a comfortable blend of these members who will return periodically to impact on family harmony.

"One of our greatest sources of discord is the inescapable family gathering," confessed Vera, one middle-aged bride of two years. "Sam and I get along beautifully until we try to plan some sort of family get-together. Then he starts with the snide remarks like, 'Bill and Yvonne smoke like chimneys—you'd think they could be more considerate in this small house.' Or, 'Does Sarah have to bring that cat with her wherever she goes? Can't she leave it at the vet's or something?' I could agree with him, but I get on the defensive and bring up a few of his son's shortcomings.

"Maybe we should give up on getting together with both families, but the kids have all been used to coming 'home' for

Christmas and Thanksgiving. Sam's son, Joe, is at college, and my Sarah has an apartment in the city near her job, so neither of them has anywhere else to go. Bill and Yvonne, my son and daughter-in-law, have no children, and Yvonne's parents are three thousand miles away. So, like it or not—and I do love seeing them—we're destined to gather on important holidays. It's a strain, though, and I have a sense of relief when they're all gone. The trouble is, I'm usually half mad at Sam by that time, thinking he doesn't appreciate my children, and I'm exhausted after being in the middle of a tense situation."

Vera and Sam's children have little in common and limited opportunity for getting to know each other. When consulted individually, each expressed a disappointment with the changes in what they each thought of as "home base."

"Sam is a nice guy and all that," Bill said, "but Mom is different with him around. She'd been alone for years, since my dad died and she always lit up when Yvonne and I came back to the farm for the holidays. When Sarah was still home, she and my mom would both fall all over themselves getting ready for us, you know, flowers in the guest room and waffles for breakfast and all that. After Sarah moved out, Mom was absolutely ecstatic when either or both of us would come home. Then she'd let us take over with a lot of the rituals, and we'd take her to church and out for a buffet brunch at the local inn. I know she needs companionship between holidays—she can't live her life around family gatherings—but, in a way, she seemed a lot happier before."

Sam's son, too, felt deprived of cherished tradition. "Pop and my mother divorced a few years ago and she remarried right away. I never could get along with my stepfather, so I moved in with Pop and—after we both survived my teenage rebellion—we developed a very special relationship. We didn't fuss much for holidays—mostly went out for meals or visited my Aunt Dot—

but we had a good time together. Had a lot of what you could call 'man-to-man' talks. Now the place is overrun with women.''

Joe looked a bit wistful as he reminisced, then shrugged his shoulders in resignation. ''You know, most of the time I'm glad Vera's there to look after Pop—he has a heart condition that kind of worries me—but when I come home I don't know exactly where I fit in.''

It is apparent that adult children have the same needs as their younger cohorts. They can feel just as displaced and have an even harder time finding their niche in the new family structure. We, as parents and stepparents, can add greatly to the harmony of family gatherings by giving each of our combined children a feeling of belonging.

Bill remembered the flowers in the guest room and the waffles for breakfast—little gestures from his mother that said ''welcome home.'' These acts of love could continue as silent reassurances, without detracting from her attention to her husband or his children.

Monica, one stepmother of older children had a construc-tive suggestion. She said, ''When I began to think of Andy's children as houseguests, I took a whole different approach to their visits. It made a pretty dramatic difference in everyone's attitude. Funny how we usually treat complete strangers (or acquaintances we don't much care for) with more courtesy than we do members of our own family.''

Monica's stepson likes Tabasco sauce with his eggs and sugar and cream in his coffee, things that the other members of the family disdain. Monica bought a tiny cream pitcher and sugar bowl especially for Mike, and he finds them with his bottle of Tabasco sauce at his place at the breakfast table. It says to him that he has a special place in the family and that his stepmother thought about him as she set the table. Monica has the sensitivity to realize that these little things mean as much to Mike as the mug with the elephant ear handles means to her grandson.

Sometimes a crisis will unite a blending family and deepen relationships between grown stepsiblings. One group of stepsiblings found themselves united in prayer as they gathered in a hospital waiting room after an automobile accident injured both parents. For weeks afterwards they cooperated in their efforts to care for the needs of the disabled couple. Even the stepgrandchildren got involved with mowing the lawn, running errands, and helping with housekeeping chores. By the time the older couple had recovered sufficiently to be independent, their children had established closer ties.

Perhaps there is nothing you can do to promote close relationships between your adult children. It is important to remember that your couple-bond is still top priority in your blending family. As part of maintaining that crucial relationship, remember to treat each other's children with courtesy and respect for their rightful places within your restructured families.

The Special Child

In our family, as in many others, the special problems of one child affected the disciplinary patterns within our home. Stephen was the oldest of our six boys. Under different circumstances, he might have been an example and a leader for the other children. But even in his early teen years, he was slipping into the dark world of schizophrenia. It was a dozen years before his disease was diagnosed and more years still before we were able to say the word aloud. But every day of the five years that he was able to live at home, his emerging symptoms affected every member of our family.

We knew that something was wrong. As time passed, it became more and more apparent that Steve was suffering from severe emotional problems. At first, when I'd come to know him as a twelve and thirteen-year-old, I'd blamed his moodiness and erratic behavior on male adolescence—something I knew little about. My own boys had not yet reached that mysterious age of puberty.

From the beginning, Steve had demanded an inordinate share of our attention. I recognized his need for love and thought that we could fill that need by providing a warm and caring atmosphere—a normal family situation, where he would be able to grow and develop in character and competence.

He was easily led and often taken advantage of by older children, who would prod him into some prank and leave him to face the consequences. Sometimes one of the other children would come home from school in tears because of his embarrassing and inappropriate behavior at school. I was struggling with my own image of our family, and I found it hard to be compassionate.

Harry and I spent long evenings talking and talking to him, while he sat silent and expressionless. The other children would tire of waiting with their own needs and creep off to bed.

Steve was emotionally unpredictable and at times could be sweet and cooperative. "Mom, I'll empty the dishwasher for you!" or, "I can make the coffee before Dad comes home." The next moment he would be exploding with temper at something, smashing his fist through a bedroom door or breaking a wooden ruler over his knee. Table tops were scratched, stereo records gouged, and dishes shattered because of his sudden mood swings.

Occasionally he would withdraw from all of us and sit sullenly by himself, staring straight ahead and resisting any communication. His erratic behavior pattern started us on a search for professional aid from a priest at the mission to a county mental health person to a private psychiatrist and back to the school counselor. No one seemed able to help. Harry was as bewildered as I. Here is a journal entry from those days:

> October 15, 1964. I had another appointment at school today about Steve. He's been smoking on campus again. What can I say? He doesn't care if he's suspended for three days or three years. He's failing most of his classes, and yet he remembers things like the length of the Cold Springs Bridge and the population of Santa Barbara. It seems like the ability to learn is there, just beneath the surface of his fragile personality, but any disciplined course of study is more than he can handle. I feel so sorry for him, sometimes, and yet I'm angry and frustrated most of the time. It's hard on the other kids, too. They try to be tolerant, but I can see them swallowing (and choking on) their anger. I'm feeling pretty hopeless about his future.

Disciplining Steve was an exercise in futility. He was not capable, we learned eventually, of anticipating consequences or learning from past behavior. He wasn't deliberately defiant, and he had some endearing qualities, but his difficulties in coping with life—and our difficulties in coping with *him*—had a profound effect on the rest of the family.

That effect could have been softened, we realize now, if Harry and I had the wisdom to seek counseling for ourselves and other family members as well as for Steve.

The Noncustodial Parent

Since things are complicated enough within our newly blending families, it is tempting to ignore the "other" parents—the noncustodial, biological mother or father of the uprooted children in our restructured household. Hopefully, the temptation will be short-lived when we realize that both our child and our blending family are best served if we can help him maintain his relationships with both his biological parents.

Professionals have found that the stability of the stepfamily will be affected by the parent without custody and his feelings about the new marriage. The children of the former marriage will tie the noncustodial parent into the stepfamily's relationship network.

In most restructured families, then, the noncustodial parent and his household will have a continuing effect on his biological child and upon the family with whom he resides most of the time.

A parent who constantly runs down his former spouse in front of their child is damaging that child's self-image. It is not hard to understand why when we remember that he is forever biologically and psychologically connected to both of his natural parents—flesh of their flesh and blood of their blood. If his dad is a "no good scoundrel," he thinks he must have some no-good-scoundrel blood of his own. Professionals have observed that the better a child's relationship with his natural parents, the better his adjustment to his stepparent(s).

One researcher reports that about one-third of the noncustodial parents lost contact with their biological children after about a year following divorce. Professionals who deal with children of divorce find that they do better when they have a continued relationship with both parents, but when circumstances have made that impossible, the custodial parent can help to counteract the effects of the child's loss.

> If a child has no contact at all with his father and no memory of him, the child is dependent upon what his mother tells him. If she speaks of the father's good qualities (she must have seen some when she married him), a boy will be able to make a positive identification with this good image of his father. But if she always refers to her ex-husband as a louse, this will give the boy a poor model to identify with, because he will come to think of himself as half a louse.[2]

If the noncustodial parent is unaccepting of the remarriage, the children involved will be torn by guilt. Allowing themselves to become part of this unacceptable group makes them feel disloyal to their parent who is on the outside.

Again, a child's self-image hinges upon positive input from both biological parents and from the reassurance that neither has abandoned him in spite of the changes in his family structure. A measure of tension and animosity is almost certain to exist between the biological parents during the time of separation and divorce. When this subsides, as it usually does with time, children become more able to adjust to the reality of their changed circumstances.

All children need consistency, concern, and limits of behavior. Membership in two families makes consistency a challenge. Lifestyle, methods of discipline, and expectations for behavior are bound to be different in every household. However, children learn quickly that rules differ under different leadership—on the school playground and in their own backyard, at Grandma's house and at church camp. So, the important thing here is that the rules within each household are consistent and that all parents are in agreement on important matters of discipline.

Dona explained her dilemma over scheduling differences between her household and that of her former husband. "Eric and his wife keep such weird hours. She works evenings as a medical transcriber at the hospital, and he works late at his print shop every night. When Bobby spends time with them, he's either alone for a couple of hours during the afternoon or downtown at the shop with Eric. Bobby and his dad go out to dinner after eight o'clock and then watch television until time to pick his wife up. Of course, it's the middle of the night before anyone gets to bed, and sometimes Bobby has to get up and go to school in the morning. It's different on weekends and holidays, but they're still used to going to bed late and getting up late. Naturally, church and Sunday school don't fit into that schedule, but I guess Bobby has to learn that everyone doesn't live the same."

Glen, Dona's husband, expressed his feelings on the subject. "I think Dona should tell Eric that Bobby needs his sleep at least on school nights. They have two cars, and his wife could drive herself home from the hospital sometimes. Another thing, Bobby is younger than my son, Josh, and he loves to brag to Josh about how he got to watch some late show on TV that I wouldn't allow Josh to watch at any hour. It's hard to explain to him why Bobby gets to watch a program that we say isn't good for kids. He wonders why the rules are different for the two of them."

"It's like in our house," Cliff volunteered. "We really keep the lid on the sweets at home. Sandy thinks too much sugar makes Brian hyperactive, and I tend to agree with her. At any rate, I've always felt that sweet snacks were just empty calories, and ruin the kids' appetite for the healthy dinners Sandy fixes. Well, Brian goes to his dad's house for the weekend and his girlfriend will show up with a batch of brownies or peanut brittle— something she thinks will please Brian—and Brian doesn't say anything. Sandy mentioned it to Gus, her ex, once or twice but he thinks she's just resenting his girlfriend."

Cliff and Sandy finally agreed to reserve their critical comments about the other household's eating habits, hoping that Brian will grow up with a preference for nutritious food instead of sweets.

"We've taught him the importance of brushing his teeth after meals, and I guess that will protect him from the cavities that sweets cause. And we expect him to be polite about whatever they serve him. After all, everyone doesn't eat the way we do, and we don't want to come off like fanatics."

Sandy and Cliff are wise in resisting the temptation to be critical of Brian's dad's household. Brian's healthy self-image is dependent upon continued respect for his father, and for his mother and stepfather to nitpick about the eating habits at his dad's house would undermine that respect.

The Wider Circle

Louise and Chuck, arms loaded with packages, slide into a booth at the mall coffee shop to take a break from Christmas shopping.

"Do you suppose Ingrid expects us to bring presents for her little girls, too?" Louise asks her husband. "After all, they have their own grandparents to send them gifts."

"We have to remember that Ingrid's daughters are part of John's family now. That makes them part of our family, as well. If we left them out, I think everyone would be offended," Chuck responds.

"I know you're right," Louise says. "I hadn't really thought it through. I wouldn't hurt John, or Ingrid, for the world. Actually, I haven't looked at dolls in ages. It will be kind of fun."

The preceding conversation illustrates one of many scenes played out within the wide circle of people affected by the blending of families. Noncustodial parents, grandparents, and other relatives may or may not accept the new family; old friends may or may not remain in their previous supporting roles. Individuals who are outside our one-roof families, but with whom we interact will have a significant bearing upon the quality of our blending family life.

When we remarry we do not blot out our previous lives and begin with a new chapter devoid of experience and memory. We have in-laws, usually, to whom we have become attached, friends who have been like "members of the family," and relatives whose relationships to us may have undergone drastic changes during the upheaval in our lives.

"I married my brother's best friend," said one young woman, "and you would have thought I'd divorced both of them. Bud used to drop in two or three times a week. But after Earl and I were separated he just stopped coming around. Even my four-year-old noticed it. He asked, 'Did Uncle Bud go to Cleveland to live with Daddy?' I told Bud he'd better knock it off and remember that I was going to be his sister forever, Earl or no Earl."

Divorce is painful enough without the loss of friends and relatives that often goes with it. When the "significant others" in our lives remain supportive, our chances for happiness and success in a second marriage increase tremendously.

"My former sister-in-law became a bone of contention between Wes and me," said Trish. "Jeanette and I had been friends forever, even before her brother and I were married. She hadn't taken sides during our divorce, and we were determined that we weren't going to let it interfere with our friendship. There were the kids, too. They'd been together a lot, as cousins, and we didn't want to break up their relationships. But Wes saw our continued association as some sort of threat to him—a link that was going to keep me connected to my first marriage. It almost broke us up.

"One day I practically dragged Wes over to Jeanette's with me. She was so open in accepting him as my future husband and a potential friend to her that it broke down some of his defenses. It's still a bit awkward, because there's always the chance that we'll run into Maynard at her house, but I'm less apprehensive about that as time goes by. We're all adults, after all, and we have to maintain a civilized relationship for the sake of the kids. I don't want them to give up their dad, and I don't want to give up my friend."

Maintaining close ties with people who have been important to our families will help our displaced children survive the changes in their young lives with a minimum of damage.

It was important to me to have my parents present when Harry and I were married. They provided a constant in the lives of my children and me. Even though they were not in complete agreement with my decision to remarry, Mom and Dad were wise enough and generous enough to realize that we needed them.

Harry set out to prove that our marital merger would be a success, and he quickly wooed my parents. Our new home brought us closer to them than we had been before, so we were able to see them more often. Grandma and Grandpa had always played a special part in the lives of my children, and their continued participation in our blending family was reassuring to all of us.

Although they were shy with their stepgrandparents at first, Harry's children responded to Mom and Dad's efforts to welcome them into the family.

Mother groaned a little at the thought of five more grandchildren to shop for at Christmas time, but she wouldn't have thought of arriving with gifts for the original four and nothing for the new family members. (To his everlasting credit, neither would my former husband. When he delivered Christmas gifts for his own children, he brought something for the new members of my family, too.)

My parents opened their hearts, as well as their purses, to include their stepgrandchildren and, in contrast to their embarrassment over my divorce, began to brag to their friends about "how well the kids are managing with that big family!" Part of the credit for our "doing well" will always belong to my parents.

They put aside their misgivings and apprehension to be supportive of us in our stubborn determination to begin a new life. We try to remember that in our dealings with our own adult children!

Thousands of miles separated us from Harry's family, but their approval and support had been obvious from the beginning of our relationship. Their encouragement from afar added stability to our restructured family. When they came for a visit, they were as attentive to my children as to their own grandchildren.

Maintaining friendships can be a problem, especially when distance enforces separation. Couple friendships will naturally dissolve when one of the couples no longer exists. Sometimes a new friendship is reestablished with the new husband or wife substituting for the former partner. However, if the couple friendship was formed because the husbands (or wives) were business associates and divorce has ended that tie, there may be little remaining mutuality to build upon.

Women are more apt to develop and value close friendships and will usually make more effort to preserve and nurture their relationships than will their husbands. During the painful upheaval of divorce or widowhood, a woman who has established a close tie with another woman may be spared from the psychiatrist's couch. Sharing her hurt with her friend can relieve her burden and speed her healing. If that friendship survives the marriage shuffle, she will have a great asset as she struggles to adjust to her new family.

"With an old friend you don't have to continually explain yourself. Some feelings are hard to put into words, and you just need someone to understand," said one recently remarried woman. "Jane knew what I'd gone through with Chad, so when I told her that Martin had gone off on a fishing trip, she knew exactly what was going through my mind. She knew I was afraid to be alone at night with the kids, and she knew why—without my going into detail. A new friend wouldn't understand without the background that Jane and I have, and that takes a long time of sharing.''

New friends, of course, enrich our lives, and many of them will become old friends eventually, but it is more likely to be an old friend to whom we turn during troubled times. These tested friendships will have a stabilizing effect upon the blending family.

A man, by nature more reluctant to lower his guard and expose his vulnerability, may deepen some existing friendships during a crisis in his life. If he can confide his frustration and fear to a friend, he will draw that person closer by his very expression of need. Most of us feel honored to be entrusted with a confidence of sought-out comfort or counsel.

Because of our move immediately after our marriage, Harry and I both left friendships that had been important to us. For a while I wrote and received letters that kept me from going over the brink into a chasm of loneliness. Occasionally, someone from "back home" might bridge the gap in our relationship with a personal visit, but our mutual interests diminished as time passed. Finally, we had to wean ourselves away from those old ties and rely more upon new friendships to fill the void.

I have talked about my friend Leslie, a kindred spirit and compassionate lady who could see through my shyness to my need. I believe that God provided us for one another—her for me, to rescue me from my isolation; me for her, to someday introduce her to the Savior who was waiting to be the true Rescuer in my life. Leslie was the first new friend in my new life, and she quickly grew to "old friend" status.

There were others. Among the people we treasured and shared as couple friends were Marlene and Jerry, a fun-loving young couple with two little girls who mixed well with our children. They brought a dimension of entertainment into our busy lives, dropping by for a game of Scrabble or bridge or inviting us (all of us!) for an informal Sunday night supper. They accepted us as we were, not caring about our checkered pasts or about whose kids were whose.

Gradually, the distinction between "his friends" and "my friends" blurred, and the number of "our friends" increased. The ones that went back to a time before our relationship began were all the more precious, because they'd survived the changes in our lives.

All of this acceptance by family and friends provided mortar for the foundation of our blending family. Family and old friends helped us to know each other better; new friendships gave us another dimension of sharing.

Young lovers often delude themselves that their twosome is sufficient in itself for happiness, then relent (especially after the first baby comes) to include their abandoned families and build a support network of new friends together. Second-time-around lovers come together with many relationships that predate their couple-bond, relationships that extend to their children and are too important to family stability to be relinquished.

"No man is an island," wrote John Donne. Neither is a couple, nor a family. God has created us to be social beings, with the capacity for love beyond the romantic.

The title of C. S. Lewis's book *The Four Basic Loves* refers to his theme. Throughout the book, he explores the differences in the basic human loves and how they are each enriched by the love of God.[4] Our hearts are designed for each facet of love, and our lives will lack in richness without them all.

8
Becoming a Family

*I*s blending really necessary?" you might ask. "Can't two people just join forces in a second marriage and get along with mutual respect and cooperation?"

Yes, perhaps we can "get along," but without the blending there cannot be the depth of intimacy that God intended for marriage. If my heart is heavy with concern for one of my children, I need to share that burden with my husband. Because he has opened himself to intimacy with my son or daughter, he can feel the pain (or the joy) of a father for his child. When we hold hands and pray together at the breakfast table, we lift *our* children in heartfelt prayer to the Lord of our lives.

Our experience and that of other combination families agrees with a statement by Tom Frydenger:

> If blending, or integration, does not take place in a reconstituted family, its members sound like two bands led by two different conductors, playing two different songs in two different keys. I have counseled blended families where each original family system insisted on playing its own song, and on playing it louder and louder in an attempt to drown the other song out. Eventually the original tune gave way to blasting noise and family discord.[1]

So far we have seen our blending family as a collection of individuals, some blood-related and some only loosely connected by the intention of two people who propose to build a new life together. Each in his own way is struggling to overcome the traumatic upheaval in his life and to find his place again. Each member, child and parent, brings his own assortment of hurts and misgivings to the fledgling family, wondering how and where he will fit in the remarriage shuffle.

To heal from the past and grow to meet the future, we must have a secure base of affection and acceptance—a *family* to whom we belong, where there is a reasonable degree of harmony and order. We survivors of divorce or widowhood need that security for ourselves, and we need to provide it for our children.

Our children have lost their original, familiar support systems—the foundation that has undergirded all of their experience and development before the dissolution of our former marriages. It is up to us to restore the security that is so necessary for further growth in responsibility and character. A blended family can be a satisfactory alternative to the nuclear family that has failed. However, "blended" is an accomplished state, and the blending is a process.

Functioning as a Unit

What, exactly, do we mean by a "blended family"? One dictionary definition of the word blend is: "to make into or become a uniform mixture." That doesn't sound much like any family I know, step or otherwise! Our goal is not to lose the wonderful variety that God has allowed in His children, but to unite our own unique combination of persons in a way that will benefit each individual and the family as a whole unit.

Another definition: "to mingle and combine so as to obscure or harmonize the varying components" more closely fits my idea of what should happen within the blending family: obscured conflicts, harmonized personalities, integration without discrimination.

People still ask me, after all these years, "Whose children are yours, and whose are Harry's?" My answer (his too, if he's asked) is that if *his* weren't mine in the beginning (and *mine* his), they certainly became *ours* over a period of time. I can't put my finger on the day or the hour when it happened for me. I began with determination to accept Harry's children as my own and somewhere along the way my mind-set became a heartfelt reality. With some—those whose personalities allowed them to lower their barriers and meet me halfway on the bridge of communication—this emotional transformation came quickly, with others more slowly.

We didn't want to think of ourselves as a "stepfamily." The use of that term brought up all kinds of unpleasant images in our minds. Because we were without a model for our blended family, our only recourse was to pattern ourselves after the natural families (especially those big, happy ones like the Waltons) that we'd admired from afar.

Our approach may have been less than realistic, but it reflected our intention to function as one family, not two fragments of families, living side by side. This goal was the cornerstone of our lifestyle. It set the guidelines for our behavior as partners and as parents.

Most parents of underaged children have a similar goal in mind as they begin a second marriage. They want to restore order to their lives and security to their children. They want another chance at a happy and successful marriage. If there is a problem, it is this: What one partner perceives as an orderly, secure family or a happy and successful marriage may not coincide with the other's picture of a goal to be sought after. Or, both partners may set their standards for family success so high that they are constantly discouraged with the reality of their progress.

I have to laugh at myself now, but my own goal was to push our motley crew into the mold of the Frank Gilbreth family as described in their fascinating book *Cheaper by the Dozen*. The Gilbreth family of twelve closely-spaced children was headed by two outstandingly brilliant and talented adults, professionals in their fields of psychology and motion study. Their training had given them exceptional skills for the management of time and people. These are not skills (I found) that one learns overnight, in the midst of chaos.

Frank Gilbreth believed that the methods he used to increase efficiency in the factory would work at home, and he organized his brood accordingly. At a family council meeting, the work of the household was allotted and apportioned on the basis of aptitude:

> The boys would cut the grass and rake the leaves. The girls would sweep, dust and do the supper dishes. Everyone except Dad would make his own bed and keep his room neat. The smaller girls were assigned to dust the legs and lower shelves of furniture, the older girls to dust table tops and upper shelves. The older boys would push the lawn-mowers and carry leaves. The younger ones would do the raking and weeding.

They chose committees to oversee the efficient operation of the household:

> Family purchasing committees, duly selected, bought the food, clothes, furniture and athletic equipment. A utilities committee levied one cent fines on wasters of water and electricity. A projects committee saw that work was completed as scheduled. Allowances were decided by the Council, which also meted out rewards and punishment.[2]

The Gilbreth children, though close in age, arrived one at a time. In addition to their capable parents, the Gilbreth clan was blessed with a cook and a handyman. In their household, according to the authors, the older kids took care of the younger ones, and the "intermediates" took care of themselves.

Minor differences, I thought. Many of their excellent ideas could be adapted to fit our family. I especially liked the one about playing Spanish or French records in the bathroom so the children could learn a foreign language while they brushed their teeth. But we could start out with Mark and Nancy polishing table legs and ease in gradually to things like that.

I found a copy of *Cheaper by the Dozen* in the local library and insisted that everyone read it and act accordingly. Our darling children humored me by taking the book to their rooms, but the results were nonexistent.

Protecting Individuality

However much we may admire another family, we cannot pattern ourselves after someone else. Each family develops its own way of coping with one another and with the outside world. The Frydengers write of a family's "unique system." Included in that system are

- the role each person plays
- the emotional climate of the home
- the way family members interact with one another and with the family as a whole
- the expectations each family member has of one another
- the way individuals fill those expectations[3]

First-marriage couples have the leisure to gradually arrive at a satisfactory compromise of ideas and philosophies upon which to base a lifestyle. We are getting a late start. Our second-marriage lifestyles will be built upon a meshing of values developed and held dear in our separate pasts. It would be ideal to explore and establish these values before marriage—before diving into the middle of things. If you have already taken the plunge without testing the waters, you and your mate could begin now to work through these questions:

1. What kind of family do we want to be? Is "togetherness" a goal? Will we share involvement as a family in community and church activities, or is it more realistic for family members to pursue their individual interests? Where can we find areas of shared interest and abilities?

2. How do we see our relationships within the family? If we want close, intimate ties, are we willing to risk being vulnerable ourselves?

3. How do we see ourselves in relationship to our "wider circle" of friends and relatives. Our neighborhood and larger community?

4. How do we want to spend our leisure time as a family? Our work time?

5. What role will religious, educational, or cultural pursuits play in our family?

6. What qualities of character and standards of behavior will we demand from ourselves and other members of the family?

7. How about traditions? Which existing ones do we keep? Shall we establish new ones? How will we deal with holidays where we may be separated?

It is good to set goals, but you should not expect the perfection of a finished product. Families are like people—in process. Sometimes it seems we are as far from becoming blended as when we started. We are constantly changing as individuals and as a family unit. These words by Maxine Hancock are an encouragement to me.

Family relationships are never—for one year, for one month, even—static. They constitute a continually adjusting relationship to the dynamic, changing people who are members of the family.[4]

Although you're starting over, you have the advantage of the added experience and maturity that accompany a second marriage. With those advantages, a few guidelines, and God's help, you can blend your family and build a life.

Following a Leader

Twelve-year-old Shauna screams at Rex, her new step-father: "Mind your own business! You're not my dad! You can't tell me what to do!"

Enter Shauna's mother. "Just let me handle it, Rex, will you? I don't think you understand." She puts a comforting arm around her daughter.

"Gladly," Rex responds, stung by his stepdaughter's rebuff and his wife's reaction. "It's high time *someone* handled Shauna. I'll just stick to supporting her!"

A few harsh words, loaded with innuendos, and this threesome is off to a rocky start. Rex's confidence in himself as a parent is shattered and he backs away from further confrontations with Shauna, who would benefit from strong guidance through her adolescence and teens.

The handling of each other's children is the number one cause of conflict in the blending family. Disciplinary problems, more than any other, can keep us from blending into a harmonious family unit.

To parent is to lead. If we can remember that the purpose of parenting is to guide, teach, and protect our dependent youngsters, and if we agree on the values and goals that will direct our course as a family, we should have an easier time finding common ground in the realm of leadership.

If Shauna's stepfather made one mistake, it was in moving too quickly to fill a role that he thought was expected of him. A stepparent must start slowly, building trust and communication before taking a place of authority in the blending family. If we want our children to submit to our leadership and accept our values, we must first convince them that we are worthy of their respect.

To do that, we must respect ourselves as leaders in the home and be reassured of our rights to that role. If parents are operating from a position of love (remembering here that love is a decision, not necessarily an emotional response), consistency, and fairness, they have a right to authority in the home.

Sometimes, because of past mistakes (and what parent doesn't make them?), we come to doubt our abilities to lead. We are inclined to add to our feelings of failure and guilt by taking responsibility for every difficulty in the lives of our children. But every problem our children have is not traceable to family upheaval, divorce, and remarriage. Growing up is hard in the best of families. Children—especially adolescents who comprise a substantial percentage of second-marriage families—are influenced by their peers, their changing bodies, significant adults outside the family, and a permissive society. As parents we have the privilege and the responsibility to discern and counteract the negatives among these powerful influences.

Children thrive in a situation where they are given loving, consistent, and reasonable leadership. In such an atmosphere, order is maintained; responsibility, developed; and character, built. Children need help in learning how to face life's challenges and meet the obligation that will grow as they mature. That's what families are all about.

When my counselor said "All you have to do is love

them," I thought he was talking about the giving of affection. But a parent's responsibilities extend far beyond that. What we want our children to learn, we have to try to teach them. To be sure, we need to teach them within an atmosphere of love, but warmth and affection are only the groundwork for instruction and guidance.

Kay Marshall Strom, in her book *Chosen Families,* reminds adoptive parents of some of a child's basic needs:

1. From infancy onward, children need good examples on which to base their own actions. They are learning constantly, and what they learn depends upon what they see.

2. Children need the love and care of an adult whom they can trust and who will give them security. Without this they will grow up severely handicapped when it comes time to form other relationships in life.

3. To develop their full potential, children need to be raised in an atmosphere of acceptance. They need to be appreciated for who and what they are.[5]

Strom is addressing the subject of adoption, but these needs apply to all children. Stepparents, take note. It is important to the child's security that the adults in his household present a united front. He has learned to trust the guidance of his natural parent, and he needs, at least at first, to feel that that parent is still in charge of his life. If his stepmother or stepfather treads softly supporting the authority that he trusts, he will gradually learn to accept that united leadership.

"I made a mistake with Brent when Phil and I were first married," said Rosalie, a young woman whose adolescent son had gone through a difficult period of rebellion during her divorce. "Brent was acting out his frustration, I see now, but I felt completely defeated by his behavior. He defied me at every turn, and I was only too happy to hand over all authority to Phil.

That just made things worse, because Brent thought I'd deserted him, along with his father, who'd left us."

The answers to this family's dilemma came through their local mental health counseling center. Rosalie was encouraged to resume her previous role of authority over her son; Phil was allowed to concentrate on building a relationship with Brent; and Brent was given an opportunity to express the fears and frustrations that were contributing to his defiant behavior.

When the following conditions prevail, a child is more likely to accept the shared leadership of his biological parent and stepparent.

- If his parents can be counted on to be fair and reasonable in their discipline.
- If his feelings are considered and respected in decisions that affect the family.
- If he understands the life-values and long-term goals that undergird his family system.

A stepparent can be guided by the biblical admonition to all parents: "Fathers, do not exasperate your children; instead, bring them up in the training and instruction of the Lord" (Eph. 6:4).

Caring, communication, and relationship come before the "bringing up." Those hurdles have to be gotten over before we've earned the right to authority over children. Those things come gradually and naturally between biological parent and child. With step relationships we start in the middle instead of at the beginning. We have no mutual history, no frame of reference from which to operate.

Christian parents have a distinct advantage in the role of discipline. The Bible contains guidelines for raising children as well as a blueprint for a successful marriage. When we can rely upon God's Word for guidance in our leadership role, we can be confident about our expectations.

God's Word says, "Train a child in the way he should go, and when he is old he will not turn from it" (Prov. 22:6).

What an opportunity we have to give our children the kind of training that God had in mind for them!

We will meet some obstacles as we assume leadership roles in our blended families. We may suddenly be confronted with the task of leading young girls, when our experience has been with boys. Or, perhaps our combined children will differ greatly in age and background experience.

Kirsten and Leonard Farmer combined his teenaged son with her two younger daughters.

"I became terribly upset by some of Kevin's behavior," Kirsten said. "The first time I found an empty beer can in our car, I demanded that Leonard confront his son and make him shape up. Len took a 'boys will be boys' approach. Kevin had just come to live with us after his mother remarried, and Leonard didn't want to rock the boat. I wasn't going to have a seventeen-year-old around who was allowed to live by a different set of rules than my little girls. We had our first big row over that."

"After we calmed down I could understand where Kirsten was coming from," said Leonard. "Of course, I didn't want Kevin to be running wild, either, but one beer can didn't seem like such a big deal. But I had to admit that we should take a stand and set some limits. The girls would be teenagers eventually, and we had to have the same rules for everyone. I think it had a positive effect on Kevin, when he saw himself as an example for his young stepsisters."

We are constantly reminded that our blending family cannot fit the familiar mold of our previous lifestyle. We are a different kind of family—one in which many of the old rules may have to be adapted to our new situation.

Consistent and loving leadership is of primary importance in the smooth functioning of our restructured family. The foundation for this kind of guidance will be as secure as the parents' marital bond, as effective as the communication between parents and children, and as authentic as the value system upon which it is laid.

Family-esteem

The concept we hold of ourselves as a family is vital to our success, as is the self-esteem of its individuals. Do we hang our heads because we came from a background of failure (as many of us did) and mentally demote ourselves to the status of second-class citizen?

"I felt like we had a sign on the front door—BROKEN FAMILY!—even after Bruce and I were married," Ellen Bailey confided. "I *knew* that I'd been forgiven—I'd come to know Christ in the interval between marriages—but I still worried about what other people thought. And I couldn't just avoid any explanation. Bruce's daughter and mine were only a few months apart, and people would ask about that. And my kids were Andersons and his were Baileys . . . there was always something."

"I know what you mean," said Janet, a member of a stepfamily support group. "But I think I was judging myself more harshly than anyone else—I don't know, maybe I'd never really accepted that forgiveness you were talking about. Anyway, my new friends and neighbors seemed to accept us well enough. And the stronger our family became *internally,* the better we felt about our *external* image."

Here are some specific things we can do to strengthen the new family.

1. **Every shared experience or activity draws us closer to one another.** Watch a funny movie together and share laughter. Plan a picnic to some unexplored place and

share the adventure. Play touch football on the lawn, charades in the family room, twenty questions in the car.

2. **Take lots of pictures of the new family and start a new photo album.** We had first-day-of-school pictures, eighth-grade graduation pictures by the front door (look how *short* I was), prom pictures with the embarrassed "dates" dragged into the living room to be posed before the fireplace.

3. **Start a new tradition for birthdays, Christmas, Thanksgiving, Groundhog Day.** On our first Christmas together, I bought red and white felt and made identical stockings to hang from the mantel—a new tradition for *our* family. Each bore a child's name, and as they married I added the name of our new son or daughter-in-law and the wedding date. Many blended families are separated during holidays because of visitation arrangements with the noncustodial parent. Most families solve that problem by arranging an early celebration—perhaps an evening at the local Christmas pageant in the park or the church cantata, followed by pizza and a drive to see Christmas decorations before gathering around the family tree for hot chocolate and gift exchanging.

As we take positive steps to tighten our bonds, we begin to feel more like a family. As we gain confidence in our marital mergers, we can hold our heads high and command respect from others. It we allow ourselves the privilege of optimism, our children will absorb our positive attitude.

Life has given us a second chance at marriage and family. It won't be perfect, but it can be better than the first, if only because of what we have learned from past failure. God's blessing and guidance are there for the asking.

9
"Where Your Treasure Is"

*A*s much as the romantics of the world (such as I) would prefer it otherwise, a lot of our time and energy seems to be directed toward "storing up treasures on earth." We live in a material world where the things that money can buy are important to us. Financial stability, or the lack of it, affects the quality of our lives. Our attitudes toward money and material possessions will have an impact upon the relationships within our blending family.

Money problems—too much, too little, too tightly or loosely held—plague most families at one time or another. In any family, arguments over how a family's income should be spent probably run a close second to those involving the discipline of its children. And in the ready-made family, financial matters can be infinitely more complicated than in the traditional, nuclear family.

Often, the budget involves child support, either coming in or going out. Either partner may have incurred debts or obligations that will be shared by the new family. Previous lifestyles and expectations for the future may differ greatly.

"Honestly, I would never have believed how *frugal* Kenneth is!" groaned Estelle. "I know it's a good trait, but he goes to extremes. If we put one extra item on our credit card during the month, we have to balance it out by cutting out all entertainment for the rest of the month—no movies, no dinners out, no nothing! He says we have to save for the future, but I thought when we got married that our future was starting now."

The economic level of the new family is rarely the same as it was for either partner in the past. Often, it is considerably lower. Sometimes the blending family is able to make ends meet on one income; in many cases both partners must work outside the home to provide the basic necessities. With the combining of families, a sudden shortage of both time and money may result. This shortage will have a direct bearing on the harmonious blending of family members.

The changing financial situation is a major area of adjustment for everyone within the blending family and needs to be faced realistically. Every couple should have some mutually agreed-upon strategy for handling money and finances. This should be more than a proposed budget. It should take into account the priorities and values that a couple holds dear. It will serve as an outline for the future—not just the "what" and "how" they will buy, but a working attitude toward life, a common understanding of what is important to both individuals.

The following guidelines are crucial in handling family finances:

- Account books should always be open to each other.
- Decisions about expenditures should be made together.
- Life values and long-term goals should be mutually held.

Many money problems that may arise can be foreseen and discussed before marriage. Honesty between the engaged partners is essential for future harmony in their home. They need to have a clear picture of each other's assets and liabilities. Following are some specific areas for discussion:

- Are there any hidden obligations or entanglements from the previous marriage?
- Will the prospective income(s) of the remarrying couple be enough to support the new family?
- Will it be supplemented by child support coming in or diminished by child support going out?
- What about insurance policies—life, health, auto, etc.? Will stepchildren be covered by existing policies? Are there restrictions that may affect the family?
- Will all assets be pooled and shared by all members of the family?
- Do the partners agree philosophically about how the available income should be spent? What habits of spending have each demonstrated in the past? Have any of these habits been a problem in the previous marriage?

Assuming that a couple has achieved a good level of communication before marriage, and that they have discovered common values and goals, they will have at least begun to make decisions about their future together. Planning monthly expenditures may be less romantic than planning the honeymoon, but it will contribute more significantly to the harmonious beginning of the blending family.

Charlie Shedd offers this guideline, "Give 10 percent, save 10 percent, live the rest."[1] That's a good place to start. If you can begin your restructured life with a mutually acceptable budget plan, you will bypass one of the hazards of second marriages.

Individual Attitudes about Money

Discussion may create dissension. Emotions simmer and tempers flare over money. We live in a materialistic society. We are protective of the "things" that we have worked hard to buy or that we value for sentimental reasons. We must come to terms with our feelings about our possessions. Do we find our security or stability or status in the things we own or in the bank accounts we harbor? Most of us do, at least in part.

Some of us use money to bolster self-esteem, to "buy" friends, or to manipulate others. It may be a temptation for the remarriage partner with the greater material wealth to use "his money" as an emotional club to control his spouse or stepchildren. We need to examine our individual attitudes about money to make decisions about the future.

For most of us, enough money means having the freedom to choose a satisfying lifestyle or to follow a dream, to improve our own lot and to contribute to the quality of life for those around us.

Each situation is different. In our family there were few decisions that weren't made for us by our circumstances. We needed a house large enough to accommodate our number, so we used all of our available cash for a down payment on the five-bedroom prefab home that we built. After buying grass seed and juniper plants and bricks for the patios, there were eleven dollars left over. I might have bought some little thing for the new house, but Harry put the money into a savings account, where it lay for a number of years, unaccompanied by further deposits.

A familiar scene at our house was Harry sitting at the dining room table after the dinner dishes were cleared, the monthly bills spread in front of him. In his meticulous way, he recorded every debt in the spiral notebook at his elbow. It was a challenge to him to see how many of our debts he could pay with our available funds. If we couldn't pay the entire sum of any bill, he would send a portion, with a note of explanation.

I would peer over his shoulder, worrying. "You'd better leave me enough for groceries and etceteras."

"What do you mean, 'etceteras'?"

"Lunch money, school pictures, student body cards, library fines for lost books, a birthday present for Nancy's friend's party, Cub Scout dues for Mark, et cetera."

He protested mildly that we were spending more than we were taking in, but he was quick to add an encouraging word.

"I know you're doing your best, honey. Don't worry, we'll make it."

I economized as well as I knew how, but I hadn't had much practice in my past life. There was no thought of my going to work. These days I see mothers of large families who are employed outside their homes, and I stand amazed at their ability to do both jobs. It took all of my faculties to fulfill my responsibilities at home. Besides, two years of a liberal arts major in college left me with no job skills that would bring in enough income to justify my working (at a paid job, that is. My fellow homemakers will understand that I "worked!").

I learned to bake bread (four loaves every other day) and sewed many of our clothes, and Harry cut the boys' hair. We had oatmeal for breakfast every school morning, because it was inexpensive and nutritious and took less milk than dry cereal. Harry was the practical one in our family, and it was his idea to subject every prospective purchase to what he referred to as the "three-way test"

1. Do we really need it?

2. Can we get along without it?

3. Can we afford it?

Usually the answers were

1. "Well. . . ."

2. "I suppose so," and

3. "I guess not."

Things like color television, soda pop, and new bedspreads failed the test, while allergy shots, track shoes, and fabric for graduation dresses made the list of necessities.

I had never been forced to live on such a restricted budget and I was secretly proud to find that I could. Harry's sense of responsibility gave me a feeling of security, and the kids seemed to adapt easily to our economic state. I worried more than they did about the changes in all our lives—my children learning to do with less and Harry's children watching their stepsiblings enjoy some extra privileges provided by their father. My children were given their own cars as they began driving and enjoyed school field trips to Mexico or Sacramento.

Child support supplemented our income, and we were grateful that my former husband, unlike many noncustodial parents, was faithful in sending his monthly check. (Only 20 percent of fathers ordered to pay child support do so regularly.)

Any dissension Harry and I might have had over money was limited by the choices open to us. I concurred with his desire to keep our bills current, and he understood my need to have enough left over for food and "etceteras." If we had had a thousand dollars left in our bank balance at the end of the month, we might have argued about what to do with it (he would have increased our savings account to 1,011 dollars!).

I have to admit to times of suppressed resentment, especially if one of *his* damaged or lost something that we couldn't afford to replace, or if one of *mine* yearned for some nonessential that wouldn't pass Harry's "three-way test." I can't pretend that we were always in complete agreement about the budget, but it was not a major area of friction in our household.

After the first lean years of our blended family, Harry left the postal service to go into business for himself as an insurance agent. That move required courage on his part and cooperation from the rest of us, as the benefits were not quickly discernible. But eventually our financial situation improved to the point where we could occasionally throw caution to the the winds and ignore our "three-way test."

Putting It All Together

In most blending families, I believe it works best to pool all assets and liabilities. Jane Bryant Quinn, syndicated columnist specializing in personal finance, says this about marriage and money:

> Ultimately, splitting vs. pooling [his and her assets] appears to be an emotional instinct, saying nothing whatsoever about a couple's attitude toward marriage. Money may be a battleground for unhappy couples. But for happy ones, anything works.[2]

Our material wealth or lack of it is a very real part of our life that we can either choose to share or withhold from one another. If we are willing to share our children, we should be willing to share our bank accounts and our property. But for some, like my friend Kay, this has been a hard decision.

Martin wanted to put his and Kay's assets in one pot from which they would pay off their debts and establish their new home. Kay's former husband had left her nearly destitute and she had struggled to put food on the table for her two little ones. Eventually she'd found a good job and, over the years, acquired a little property of her own. She was understandably afraid to release what she felt was a guarantee of security.

"I know Marty won't run out on me like Preston did," she told their pastor, "but it seems reasonable enough to keep a small account—maybe just a part of my income—in my own name. I don't need to bother Marty about every little thing I want or that I'd like to do for my kids."

"But that's like dividing our family from the beginning," Martin protested. "It makes me feel that Kay doesn't trust me to provide whatever she needs. And I want to join in the 'doing for the kids'—I always thought that was a father's place, and I want to become a father to them."

When Kay understood that Martin meant her to have a free rein with their joint account (a privilege lacking in her first marriage) and that she wouldn't be expected to ask permission for every little expenditure, she conceded to his wishes.

David Hocking, counselor in the field of divorce and remarriage says,

> You must forget the past and commit yourself totally to your new relationship. If you can't do that, it is better that you not remarry until you are able to make such a commitment. Remarriage is starting all over again. In order to do it right, the old attachments and agreements must be broken, and new ones established. Every married couple must be sure that there are "no strings attached" and "no loopholes" to their commitment. Take the words "what if" out of your vocabulary. Have no "plan B" in case your "plan A" doesn't work. Burn all your bridges and do all you can to build the unity and interdependency of your new marriage relationship. With the Lord's help, you can do it.[3]

"No!" a young mother protests. "I believe my first responsibility is to the children God placed in my care. That attachment cannot be broken nor that bridge to their father burned. I want my second marriage to be a good one—I hope this time is forever—but I have to be realistic. Marriages fail every day, as my first one did. I have to protect my children."

This woman hung on to her "independence fund," as she called it, with her husband's blessing.

"If it makes her feel better, it's okay with me," he said

with a shrug. "I make enough to take care of our everyday expenses."

In each of the above cases, one partner was able to yield to the perceived need of the other.

The Child Support Tangle

Child support, intended to ease the burden for the parent who has custody of children, can create a sticky situation in the blending family. Consider the following situation.

Allen, Eva's husband, sends a monthly check for the support of his children, who live with their mother. To make ends meet, and to compensate for this continuous drain on the family budget, Eva took a job outside the home. She feels that she is neglecting her own children (whose father has moved beyond the reach of the law and avoids any responsibility for them) to support stepchildren who take her for granted.

"I dread every visitation period," Eva confessed. "It makes me feel terrible because I really wanted to support Allen in his relationship with his kids. But they can be downright hateful. I just look at them and think of what they're costing me—not just in having to work, but in time lost with my own kids. And after awhile, I begin to resent Allen as well as his bratty kids."

This particular marriage was so stressed by the changes in family structure and routine and by Eva's resentment that it almost ended in divorce. In desperation the couple sought counseling from the pastor of a local church.

"We almost gave up on our marriage," Eva said. "I see now that it wouldn't have had to go that far. I was exhausted from all the changes in my life, and I didn't want to admit to myself that remarrying was anything but a positive step. My family had given me all these dire warnings about how hard it was going to be, so I kept insisting everything would be wonderful if it weren't for his kids. Well, of course, it was hard. I exaggerated everything his kids did, and I transferred my self-pity to sympathy for my kids. Pastor Petersen helped me see all that. Probably the biggest mistake I made was in not being honest with Allen about my feelings. He was so understanding, and he found there were things he could do to help compensate for my having to work—like taking his kids out somewhere when they come to visit and giving me a little breathing space. He was glad to help me with the weekend chores, too, once he understood my frustration with lack of time.

"Actually we've all benefited from finding ways to cope with a difficult situation. And getting to know the pastor was just the nudge we needed to start going to church again. We take all the kids, when his are with us, and go out for pancakes after the service. It's our first all-family tradition. I can be more relaxed because I'm not waiting on everyone, and I've caught myself actually enjoying Allen's kids more than once. I know I exaggerated their faults, or maybe they just improved as I settled down."

Incoming child support can create just as much havoc in the blending family as outgoing payments. Unless all living expenses are provided by the head of the household, the support check will either go into a second account or be absorbed into the family funds.

"Our pastor advised us to put all our assets in one pot," said Arnita, "but I felt that a disproportionate amount of our budget was going to Rob's three children, when almost half of our income was being provided by my former husband. It was a touchy subject, and I hated to say anything—Rob was certainly doing his best for everyone—but when my Jill couldn't buy a new prom dress because his Robbie needed braces, I protested."

Arnita and Rob sat down with their pastor and rehashed the

family finances. Rob admitted that he'd felt guilt about taking any of another man's money to help with the expenses of his own children, but that he felt trapped in a difficult situation.

There was no easy answer. For this couple, a suggestion from their pastor appealed to both of them. They agreed to give Jill—Arnita's only child and the family's only teenager—an allowance for clothing and "extras" out of her father's monthly check. She was delighted, and her stepsiblings were enough younger that they didn't view her allowance as an unfair privilege or unequal treatment.

Arnita and Rob saw that better communication might have led them to the same solution earlier in their marriage, and they vowed to be more open about their feelings in the future.

Disneyland Dads

Jenny called Dick a "Disneyland Dad." "It's not the child support check going out that's the problem in our house. I get one from my ex-husband, and it kind of evens out. But Dick travels fifty miles every Friday afternoon to pick up his son, takes him out for a fun evening, and then brings him home for the weekend. If Brandon gets whiney while he's here, which he usually does—he's pretty babyish for a seven-year-old—Dick bribes him with promises of ice cream on their way home, or they'll stop to buy baseball cards or something. The weekends get pretty expensive. I usually cook something special too—he's such a finicky eater. Once Brandon didn't like what I'd fixed, and Dick bought him a hamburger on the way home. That really upset me!

"My kids, a boy and a girl, are eight and ten, and they don't get any of this special treatment. Their dad lives in another state and wouldn't take them for the weekend if he lived next door. I think they should have a little money spent on them once in awhile. Dick is so generous with me—I can buy anything for myself, but when it comes to Linda or Larry, it's a different story."

Financial matters within the blending family can be complex. But the hurdles we encounter can be minimized and overcome if the couple-bond is strong and the communication is kept flowing. Remarrying couples need to look at their financial circumstances realistically and pace their lifestyle accordingly. Our bank accounts will affect the quality of our lives, like it or not. That is reality.

"Keep your lives free from the love of money and be content with what you have, because God has said, 'Never will I leave you; never will I forsake you'" (Heb. 13:5).

10
Sharing

What is the magic that knits together the members of a family? Is it the blood connection, the biological link, or is it the moments and experiences shared over the years?

My brother and I rarely see each other in these middle-aged years. We lose track of the things that are happening to one another today, even this year, but we are forever linked by the ghosts of our mutual past. As little children we built castles in the sand together, as teenagers we whispered secrets of our first loves to one another, and as adults we've shared the joy of coming to know Jesus Christ as our separate paths brought us to a mutual faith.

We shared roots but, more important, we shared time and space and experience.

Stepsiblings have been uprooted from their family of origin and transplanted to another growing place. There is an initial shock. But, like tender plants, children can adapt and flourish and grow with loving care. As they grow together, their roots will intertwine and their branches mingle.

Sharing Experiences

In the beginning, the blending family may share little aside from the stress of upheaval. But there are some positive aspects to the old adage "misery loves company." Stepsiblings have been known to draw close to one another as they commiserate.

If you have ever felt lost in a new situation and then found another confused soul wandering around, you know how much strength there is in companionship. You might not have chosen that particular person as a friend under ordinary circumstances, but you are apt to overlook the lack of any common bond as you join forces in a quest for security. As you give encouragement to another, you find a reserve of courage within yourself.

The same philosophy holds true for two strangers in a hospital room with nothing more in common than apprehension of the next day's surgery. We are driven to reassure one another, and when our own ordeal is over, we will want to know how our roommate fared. Caring comes from sharing, and we draw closer to one another in the trenches of life's battlefield.

Lifelong friendships are made in neighborhoods, especially new housing tracts, where neighbors collaborate to build fences and plant lawns. As two women hang curtains at bare windows, they smile and wave from one house to another. Their husbands pause in their landscaping chores for a moment of conversation about sprinkler systems and fertilizer. These people are making themselves at home in their chosen corner of the world, finding their places in a world of newness.

It is the same in a restructured family. Each member looks for ways to fit into the new situation. Our children, in their initial insecurity, are drawn closer to others in the same boat. They may feel strange and lost, but it eases their pain to realize that they are not alone.

To live in a family is to share. Stepsiblings, as unlike as roses and rutabagas, suddenly find themselves sharing things like

- closet and drawer space (reluctantly)
- dishwashing detail
- a giggling session over a TV comedy
- a mutual dislike for Brussels sprouts
- the discovery of a "climbing" tree in the backyard
- dread of the seventh-grade math teacher
- parents

One ordinary day of shared experience follows another until eventually there are shared memories. That is the glue that bonds members of a family.

Nancy and Harry Jr. came a step closer to each other on an ordinary day. They each had special love for our family pet, a toy poodle who answered to "Pierre." He was no lap dog, but a sturdy little thing who beat a daily path through the field to see his girlfriend, Sugar, and came home with foxtails in his ears. He was officially Nancy's dog, having been a Christmas gift from her father, but Harry Jr. (in defiance of his allergies) had formed a tighter friendship with Pierre than with some of his siblings. Harry Jr. and Nancy had little in common in those early days, but they both loved Pierre, and they were both home with colds the day he was run over and killed. The three of us wept together, and the two children consoled each other in their mutual grief.

Tears, laughter, excitement, joy, sadness, boredom—the emotions that ebb and flow within a family as month follows month strengthen and stabilize the ties between us.

Sharing Memories

We began our family as individuals who had come together from different worlds. There was no shared history between

Harry's family and mine. There were no "remember whens" between our two sets of children. But memories began with our first hour of sharing and built from that day forward.

Wouldn't it be nice if we could remember that every hour is a tiny piece in the jigsaw puzzle of our lives? If we did remember, and could control ourselves to act accordingly, we might (in our old age) look back on brighter pictures of our past, glowing with happy memories. Human nature being what it is, most of us will settle for a good measure of colorful moments that stand out against a darker background. Treasured memories are like that. They light up our lives like the reds and yellows in the puzzle. As we look back, we focus on our shining hours and let the duller ones fade to the edge of our memory.

I didn't know there would be so little time in our blended family life while the children were still at home to create and store up memories. Some of those hard years seemed to drag along at the time they were happening. Now, looking back, they sped by. Most parents of grown children find that to be true.

I sit at my desk and look around at the rogue's gallery on the walls. Faded snapshots of our wedding with our children clustered around; then a picture my dad took of our new family in front of our first Christmas tree (what a scraggly thing it was, propped on boxes in a bare corner of the room). There are "first-day-of-school" pictures when the kids lined up on the back step in their new outfits (I can almost hear someone saying, "Hurry up, Mom, the guys are waiting!"). Graduation pictures take up a wide section of the wall, followed by wedding portraits, family picnics, and—can it be?—sixteen grandchildren, whose pictures (no more 8x10s, please!) extend to the corner of the room. An abbreviated history of our blended family. Fragments of precious memories.

A lot of the memory-making happened automatically, but much of it was a deliberate attempt by us to promote togetherness within the family. Because money was scarce, we looked for inexpensive or free activities in which everyone could become involved.

In the fall, high school football games were great opportunities for family outings. The team players and most of the spectators were strangers to us at first, but the Friday night games drew many local valleyites. Our children would meet their schoolmates and cavort on the sidelines while we rooted for the home team.

With blankets and jackets for the crisp evenings and a huge picnic supper for half-time, we took our place in the boosters' section, cheering the local athletes on to victory. There were some good natured moans and groans from other spectators as we crowded into the bleachers with our equipment, but the sounds of, "Look out, here come the Johnsons!" made us feel at home and affirmed the validity of our family.

Missed Sharing

Holiday celebrations and family vacations are wonderful memory makers, but in a blending family they can often be divisive.

My friend Shirley talked about her family's summer vacations. "It seems as if the very things that could have brought my daughter and Pat's closer together separated them instead. Michele and Francie would just be beginning to develop a sisterly relationship when Francie would be whisked off for the summer to visit her dad and stepmother out West. Michele would be unenthusiastic about going on vacation without Francie so we'd let her take a friend. When Francie came home, Michele would be thick with the new friend—they'd sit around and giggle about their summer romances and Francie would feel left out and understandably envious of the fun she'd missed.

"Francie could have rearranged her visits with her dad, but she was torn. She didn't want him to think anything else would be more important than their time together. The girls did get to spend Easter vacations together, going to church camp with the youth group, and those times gave them a special bond."

Our family, too, was usually divided during summer vacations. While my children visited their father, Harry and I took the rest of the family camping at the beach. It was a memorable time for all of us—fun for the kids and a respite for me—but there was always that wistful regret that my absent children were missing this happy time. It was the most relaxed and carefree time of the year, a time when Harry and I could let down and just have fun with the kids.

We were fortunate to have everyone together for the major holidays. Our children share Christmas morning memories of rising early to peer at the shadowy forms around the darkened tree and the newly-bulging stockings straining at their pegs on the mantel. They huddled on the cold stairs until sounds from our bedroom sent them scuttling back to their warm beds to wait for the crackling of a wood fire and the reflected glow of Christmas lights, dancing in the stairwell to call them to the celebration.

One Thanksgiving my courageous mother invited all of us to dinner at her house. Friend Leslie offered their station wagon, and Harry and I each drove a carload—five youngsters in one car, four and Pierre in the other, with the kids communicating by walkie-talkie on the three-hour drive. That was the year that one heating element of mother's oven died, and she had to "broil" the poor turkey, one half at a time, with nine hungry children peering over her shoulder. On another holiday at Grandma's house, my sister-in-law baked a pumpkin pie that has never been forgotten in our family. I think it was called "citron surprise." One of the kids dubbed it "citron shock" after sneaking his piece out to the kitchen and burying it in a mound of turkey bones. We still giggle at the memory of trying to act polite as we each dallied with the offensive mixture on our plates. Those kinds of memories—the funny things that happened on our way to growing up—enrich our family today.

An Error

There is one area of family sharing that I would handle differently, if I could change the past. It has to do with sharing bedrooms.

When we moved into our new house, we assigned our six boys to the three bedrooms and two bathrooms on the upper floor. It seemed fair to give the largest bedroom with its adjoining bath to the oldest boys, Steve and Chris, and the smallest bedroom to the youngest. That put Tom and Harry Jr. in the middle bedroom and Mark and Greg (natural brothers who had been together always) in the smallest bedroom. As the older boys left home the rest would spread out, each having his turn at the more desirable rooms.

We were still perplexed about Steve's erratic behavior and thought that Chris, compassionate and tolerant by nature, would be a good influence for him. Instead, Chris quietly endured a situation that must have been difficult for him.

Many years passed before both Chris and Tom expressed their disappointment in having been separated in our new family. As adults, they have lived in different parts of the country, and they regret the days when they could have been closer as brothers. In trying to be fair and to equalize the privileges among the boys, we made a poor decision. Steve was not benefited, and we sacrificed the quality of a relationship between two brothers.

Sharing the Work Load

By simple mathematics, the increased number of people in a restructured family will increase the demands upon us as parents. We want to create and maintain a comfortable home. As we give our children a part in the planning and carrying out of this necessary work, they will increase their feelings of self-worth. As they learn and become competent in basic skills, they grow in independence. As they work alongside their siblings and parents, they gain a sense of belonging that no reassuring words can give them. Sometimes there are major adjustments to be made in the work habits of the parents before things begin to run smoothly in the restructured household.

Before his marriage to Ruth, Mitch lived in a bachelor apartment, coming home in the evening to a lifestyle that was lonely but uncomplicated by lawns to be mowed or children waiting with broken bicycles or Cub Scout projects.

"That was one of the hardest things for me," said Mitch. "I wanted a home and a family, but I just wasn't used to the demands those things included. My job was physically taxing, and my body was programmed for rest when I came home at night. Yet the work had to be done, and I wanted to get off to a good start with the kids. They really needed my help."

"Mitch was great about pitching in and helping with the kids' projects," said Ruth, "but I could see that we all needed to make some concessions. With extra laundry and cooking (The kids and I had gotten pretty casual about meals.), I had more work in some departments, but Mitch was taking on a big part of my burden of yard work and helping the kids with things I wasn't good at. Heather and I took on the job of washing the cars, and Lance got out and helped Mitch with the lawns."

Sharing the necessary work of the blending family is an opportunity for the step relationships to develop and grow.

Again, I speak mostly from hindsight wisdom. Many times it seemed easier to do something ourselves than to enlist the help of a reluctant child. A typical exchange in our household went something like this.

"Greg, would you come up and take out the garbage?"

"Aw Mom, I've got my shoes off!"

"Well, put them on."

"Can't I wait until the next commercial? Anyway, I did it last time. It's Chris's turn."

I had my shoes on and I was a lot closer to the garbage can anyway, so I'd capitulate. Often though, I'd swallow my resentment, which would leak out later in little spurts of irritability or sarcasm. I see that now. The kids were resisting like normal kids. In not persevering I was cheating them of their rightful growth in feelings of competence and self-esteem. Our family work load was large enough for everyone to share.

I don't mean to infer that our children were uncooperative. They did help, especially in an emergency (Grandma and Grandpa coming for Christmas, for instance). The older girls, in particular, shared the never-ending kitchen chores, while the boys pulled weeds and swept the garage when they were asked. But our time for togetherness, which in retrospect went too fast, could have been stretched and enriched if we had found more opportunity to work together. And in working together, we would have created more time for playing together.

Sharing People

Perhaps the most binding element of all in a restructured family is the sharing of people. Old relationships are broadened to include new members of the family. Aunt Bessie becomes aunt to her stepnieces as well as to her "blood" kin. New friends come into our lives, and they are "our" friends, blind to any division of people within the family. Our boundaries are extended into a wider circle. As the years pass, the dividing lines within our family fade. We've had some "crossovers" that have become symbols of our "blending."

One of our family treasures is my late father's eyewitness account of the San Francisco earthquake and fire. He was barely fifteen in 1906, and the bricks were still falling when he penned his description of that historic event. When it came into my possession at his death, I made copies for all of our children, thinking it would have significance for the grandchildren and their future descendants. It was Harry Jr., stepgrandson, that picked up the ball, walked the streets of San Francisco with his journalist mind mapping my dad's escape route from his ruined boardinghouse to the old ferry building. He researched and annotated the old manuscript and entered it in the San Francisco History Fair, where it received second prize. Eventually it was picked up and published by *California History* magazine where "shirttail" relatives as far away as Connecticut read it and were pleased.

There have been other incidents, too. Nancy, attending seminary and far away from home at Christmas for the first time, braved icy roads to spend a snowy Christmas with Grandma Johnson, her stepgrandmother in Wisconsin. In Harry's mother's last years, it was Nancy who, with her pastor husband, was near enough to visit the nursing home and represent the rest of the family at the funeral.

Sharing Spiritual Life

In many blending families, there is little or no structured religious dimension. Often, both segments of the new family have come from different denominations or have become estranged from their individual churches during their single lives.

Many church bodies neglect to adequately support their divorcing members, and many "singles" have a difficult time fitting into their church's congregation. If the newly blending family can find a church home in which they are comfortable, they will increase their chances of successful blending tenfold.

Our family had a problem in that area. Both Harry and I had married spouses whose religious doctrine forbade divorce. They were both Catholics, living in different cities, and had taken the lead in the children's religious training. Neither Harry nor I had had any definite religious convictions (outside of a rather vague faith in God), so we had left that department to our former spouses.

Because we wanted to keep the changes in our children's lives to a minimum (and we didn't have any better ideas), we encouraged them to continue their catechism classes in our new community. We went through the motions of going to church as a family a few times, but we were less than comfortable in a congregation where divorce is unacceptable. Finally, we solved our discomfort by providing transportation to and from church until they were old enough to drive themselves. We made virtually no attempt to participate in their spiritual life. It was a poor arrangement and an unsatisfying one, but Christ was yet to become the center of our lives.

All of our children were confirmed in the church and several married within that faith, but none have retained their affiliation with that denomination as adults. I have come to believe, from our experience, that young people will not find deep and lasting significance in any "religion" that is inherited as a tradition and reserved for Sundays and weddings. It was our place to be spiritual leaders in our home, but we couldn't teach what we hadn't learned ourselves.

As I've said, Harry and I wanted God's stamp of approval on our marriage and on our family. If it couldn't come to us through the only church with which we were acquainted, we thought it must be out of our reach. It wasn't, of course. I believe the Lord honored our desire and waited patiently for us to open our hearts to Him.

We are active in a church today where many young families hear God's Word spoken on Sunday morning and enjoy fellowship together during the week. Their children attend Sunday school and youth groups and hold car washes and bake sales to make money for summer camp and winter ski weekends. Some of these families have single parents and some are remarrieds, in one stage or another of the blending process. I envy them the place they have found, and I applaud their acceptance within our congregation.

Is it "better late than never" for us? Of course. Harry and I have become united in spirit as we've discovered a faith we can share. Our acceptance of Christ as Savior and Lord of our lives has given our marriage a dimension that was lacking in our first marriages. Whether or not our faith and our lifestyle have a significant influence on our adult children, we are confident that God hears our prayers for them.

Our Stephen is one whom God has blessed with His gracious gift of faith. God broke through the mental confusion that will plague our son forever, perhaps, and disclosed Himself to Steve one dismal night as he stood outside the board and care facility where he lives.

"I *knew*, I just *knew* that God loved me and that Jesus died for me," he told us. "And I went in and lay on my bed and cried. Wasn't that funny, Mom and Dad?"

Funny? That's amazing grace in action. And more than ever, we believe in miracles. Steve's faith is simple. Most sermons are too long and complicated for his limited power of concentration. But I'll bet the angels sang an extra chorus when our handicapped son came into the fold, and I know his prayers are a sweet, sweet savor to God.

Sharing the Future

As the months and years go by, our blending families will almost automatically become knit together. We may begin with only our brokenness in common, but as we share space and time and experience, we narrow the gaps between us.

Those of us whose blended pasts sped by too quickly can be encouraged as we anticipate a vast future to be shared with our continuously blending, ever-extending family. We share in the joys of a daughter's newborn baby, a son-in-law's restored health after open-heart surgery, a grandson's victory in a local poster contest. Telephone wires hum between states when there is a family triumph or crisis. Every holiday brings opportunity for added sharing and tighter bonding.

Each day is another brick toward the building of a mutual history. Somewhere along the line we will discover that we have, indeed, become a real family.

11
The Younger Generation Looks Back

What have we achieved after years of the blending process? Has it all been worth it?

I have talked to many adults from blended-family backgrounds. Some interviews were formally arranged and conducted; some, triggered by such offhand remarks as "You've been in Georgia? My stepfather lives in Georgia."

Most of us veteran blenders are happy with our marriages as they stand today (perhaps because the less promising mergers dissolved within the first few years). Some are ecstatic; others have only endured. Jennifer is a good example of the former.

"I grew up in a big Italian family, where our blood ties seemed to mean a lot. Our house was always overflowing with aunts and uncles and cousins and grandparents. That was my picture of what a family ought to be. My first marriage was a disaster. My husband resisted my family's attempts to bring him into the fold—he didn't even like to do 'family' things with our own kids. He was into ham radio and retreated to his backyard 'ham shack' whenever there were more than two people in the room. Sometimes he'd go for days without speaking to me or the kids.

"My life now with Wayne has been so different. He adores

my parents and relatives and can't get enough of them. My little old grandma lives down the street, and Wayne insists on bringing her up here for dinner at least once a week. He's been like a connecting link between my kids and their extended family. Whatever hurt they had (and I had, too) at the breakup of my first marriage has been more than compensated for by the wonderful family life we have now. I couldn't be happier."

Those whose experiences have been less satisfying say,

"I'm no better off in this marriage than in my first. It's been a struggle all the way. But now that the kids are grown the hardest part is over, and I couldn't survive another divorce."

Or,

"Well, I wouldn't do it over again. It was too hard on the kids. I think I sacrificed them to a dream that couldn't come true."

So how *have* our children fared? Have we "sacrificed" them? As my pragmatic husband would say, "The proof is in the pudding," the "pudding" being, in this case, our grown children and the adult children of other families like ours. They can look, finally, with a mature perspective at the life from which they have come—a life that we chose for them, sometimes in spite of their protests and tears. We chose because we were the adults then, with the power of authority.

Today, after the fact, we see our children as young adults, facing some of the same conflicts that shaped our lives in the past. Have we given them the coping skills they need to face a difficult world? Did our choices, centered in our own need for another chance at a happy marriage, help strengthen or damage their developing characters?

*   *   *

Howard Jenkins, a fortyish lawyer, shared his story.

"My sister and I were eleven and twelve when our father died. He'd lost a leg in World War 2 and came out of the service a bitter and defeated man. I have no memory of him ever smiling and laughing. He was an alcoholic, and that's what killed him, though no one ever talked about it. Mother divorced him a couple of years before he died—no one talked about that either, or about the remarriage. Sis and I just found ourselves in a new family one day when we were young teens. My mother married more from loneliness than for love, I think. My stepfather was a hard man to like, let alone love.

"Mother acquired three small stepsons when she married—the youngest only two. They'd lost their mother after an automobile accident that left her bedridden for a year before she died. All of the children—including my sister and me—were emotional basket cases.

"Both families came from a great deal of hurt, and there had been no healing. In those days, or at least in our family, no one even thought to talk about what sort of hurts were occurring. Maybe some kind of family therapy could have helped. I think everyone used up their emotional strength just trying to survive. Both families suppressed feelings, but they bubbled up in anger and frustration and illness.

"All of us kids had so many unmet needs. Sis was the only girl and filled with rage at her circumstances. She had no private space. Her bedroom was little more than a hallway next to our parents' room. Our little stepbrothers and our demanding stepfather took all of Mother's time. Sis was expected to pitch in and help with the cooking and cleaning. She rebelled. I don't see that she ever became a part of the new family unit. She only endured. It has taken a real toll on her life.

"Things weren't so bad for me. I buried myself in school and sports and managed to do well in both, which pleased my mother. I was the oldest, too, which gave me a special place in the family. I ignored my stepfather, so he pretty much left me alone.

"I can't say our family really 'blended,' but our parents did stay together, and now there's a kind of family unit. We see each other at weddings and funerals. Mother always felt inadequate to cope with her stepsons and a difficult husband, but she did a pretty good job. My stepbrothers think she's great.

"We're probably all carrying some emotional scars from our backgrounds, but I guess the adults did the best they knew how. I think my childhood experiences make me value my own family today more than I might otherwise."

*   *   *

Pamela Morgan, an attractive, soft-spoken young woman of about thirty-five, expressed her feelings about her blended background and "the only real negative in our family."

"When my mother left my real father, who was a professional man, she left a standard of living that we children had taken for granted—one much higher on the social and economic scale than the one we experienced with my stepfather. I didn't think so much about it then, but now I look back at some of the things I missed out on. Probably I grew more as a person in that small town that we moved to—it was a little melting pot of many income levels and ethnic groups—but I find myself envying the social poise of the people I see in my dad's world.

"I gained a sister with whom I've always had a close relationship, and that's been a real plus. My stepfather—we all called him 'Pop'—was good to us. He's kind of a low-keyed personality, so he didn't come on with some strong, authoritative role that probably would have caused me to rebel. Even so, we were bound to miss out on some of the things my real dad could have done for us—material and otherwise."

*　　*　　*

"Blended families?" Vivian Black almost spat the words as we talked about her own childhood. "Ours wasn't blended in any sense of the word. Oh, my stepmother was nice enough to us for the first couple of years after she and my dad were married—I was seven then and a pretty lonely little girl—but once they had a baby of their own, my brother and I were practically ignored. My dad just went along with everything she did, and I've never been able to forgive him for that. I left home as soon as I could make it on my own. Now my husband and our kids are my family. We took them all back to Iowa once, thinking the kids should get to know their grandparents and vice versa, but it was a disaster. Zola—that's my stepmother—wasn't even nice to my little boys. Dad half-apologized and said Zola was having 'nervous spells,' but I'm not going to bother to go back again."

*　　*　　*

"I adored my stepmother," said Maureen. "I remember my own mother very well, and I was heartbroken when she died. I was about nine then. My dad married a friend of our family, and I know I had some idea in my mind that my mother had picked Pearl specifically to be my new mother. Mom and Pearl were school chums, and Pearl used to get teary-eyed when we talked about my mother. Before she passed away last month, Pearl gave me some pictures of herself with Mother when they were children. I have a feeling they had a reunion in heaven and Pearl told my mother all about her life with us."

*　　*　　*

Mary Jo was on her own and no longer lived at home when her father remarried.

"I was twenty-one and married when my mother died, but I hadn't really weaned myself away from my family yet, and it was a terrible shock when I lost Mom. I flew home for her funeral in the spring and back again at Christmas to meet my new stepmother.

"My grandparents were incensed at my father's haste in remarrying, and my brother was bitter. Our old family friends wouldn't accept my stepmother and stopped coming around. That holiday was *dismal!*

"I put my own grief on hold and tried to make peace with the two stepsisters I found in my old bedroom and the woman who was taking my mother's place. Somehow I felt responsible to make everything all right, when I probably should have been resolving my own emotions.

"Eventually we 'blended' pretty well, in spite of the obstacles. My stepsisters and I have worked to develop good relationships, as women will. My brother has little to do with the family. I have grown close to my father. My stepmother has outgrown her jealousy over my mother, and that has helped our relationship. She has worked very hard to grandparent my children and to treat all of us equally. I appreciate her efforts. We are very unlike each other (I'm sure we wouldn't have chosen each other as friends.), but her life echoed in my life has taught me a lot. I value my relationship with my stepsisters. They have extended our family, and we are all better for it."

* * *

From a pleasant, mild-mannered young man who had come in to repair our furnace. "Yeah, I have a stepmother. I hate her. I've hated her since the day she came into my life. She had her own kid about my age who could do no wrong. He's turned out to be a no-good bum, in and out of jail, while I'm going to school and working for my dad and trying to make something of myself. He's a great guy, my dad. I don't blame him for anything. But it's no big deal. I never knew my real mother, and you don't miss what you never had."

*   *   *

Patsy White shared her unusual experience. "My mother died when I was seven and my father married again a couple of years later. My stepmother was truly a blessing. She rescued me from a time of sexual abuse by my father. The memory of those years alone with him was so awful that I blocked it out of my mind for a long time afterward. I don't know if my stepmother ever suspected, but she was a wonderful mother to me and I grew to love her. As an adult I'm a lot closer to her than to my dad. We've never talked about the things that happened and probably never will. When I became a Christian I needed to forgive him, but there's a barrier between us. I'm really grateful for my stepmother."

*   *   *

"My mother left me when I was six months old, and my grandmother cared for me until my father married Bernice. They had five kids together, one after another, and I was just old enough to be a convenient babysitter. I felt that my only value was in my usefulness—that the younger children were the important ones in the family.

"All the time I was growing up I prayed that my own mother would come back to get me, dreaming that my life would be perfect then. I was twenty-five when I finally met her, and my disappointment was overwhelming. I realized then that she'd left me because she didn't want to be bothered with a baby, not for any mysterious reason that I'd fantasized. All those years I'd held my father and stepmother at arm's length, saving my love for my mother, who never wanted it. I found out too late that my dad and stepmother—and my grandmother—were the ones who really cared about me. My disillusionment hurt, but it gave me a different perspective, and it brought me closer to my 'real' family. That's been an added joy in my life the last couple of years."

*   *   *

"My parents were both alcoholics, and I guess our home life was a mess, although I was too young to remember. They split up and left my brother and me with an aunt and uncle. My mother disappeared, but my father eventually straightened up, married again, and retrieved us. By that time I was happy where I was and didn't want to go, but no one asked me. My stepmother had a couple of kids of her own, and of course she was partial to them. I don't know how my life would have turned out if I'd stayed with my aunt and uncle. I might have had a happier childhood, but I'm okay now. I have a nice family of my own."

*   *   *

"I know that my mother was better off after she and my father divorced. He was a traveling salesman with a girlfriend in every port. The whole town knew it, and it got back to us by little subtle remarks people would make. Even so, it was like our family had 'status' as long as our father was in the picture and came home once in awhile.

"We were a big family. My mother had to work to make ends meet, and we were pretty disorganized in our lifestyle. We lived in an upper middle-class neighborhood, and it was pretty obvious that the neighbors looked down on us. I felt like we were a flawed family.

"Mom married again a few months after the divorce. I was a teenager, and at that point my stepfather was just one more thing for me to rebel against. I was pretty mixed up for a while. Elmer had several kids of his own who came to visit now and then. He was a nice guy, and his kids were nice enough, but we never 'blended.' They were so *different* from my brothers and me, in interests, looks, everything. We were education-oriented and they were into motorcycle clubs and things like that. I don't think you can blend families like ours.

"But I think I've gained from growing up around so many different kinds of people. I have more understanding and compassion for others than a lot of my friends do."

*   *   *

"My mother was better off, for sure, without my dad browbeating her all the time. In a way I was relieved when they separated. He was a real tyrant with her—gentle with us—but she never could live up to his expectations, and his constant criticism defeated her. She married a guy who thought she was terrific, and I think that changed her whole personality. We kids suffered, though.

"I wonder a lot of times if my parents couldn't have worked it out. My wife and I have hit some rough waters in our marriage, but we muddled through for the sake of the kids. I'm not sure I go along with the theory that says a bad marriage is bad for kids. Every marriage is bad sometimes. Divorce hurts kids, always. I guess it's a mixed bag though. I sure wouldn't have wanted to watch my mother's unhappiness year after year."

*　　*　　*

"My stepfather didn't have an easy job. My mother helped me become aware of that early on, after I'd said something to my stepdad that hurt his feelings. She made me realize that our new family situation wasn't easy for him either. Dad (we called him that) was always fair with us—never tried to force himself in his father role. I've grown to admire and respect him.

"I was fortunate to spend time with my 'real' dad. He came for a visit at least once a month, and we stayed with him for a month in the summer. I loved spending time with him, but it was sometimes difficult to balance my relationship with him in the context of the new family. While I was trying to adapt to a new family, I was constantly reminded of the old one that lay broken on the ground. I felt guilty in my ambivalence, as if embracing one meant discarding the other. I couldn't discuss it with either parent for fear of the way it might have made them feel. To this day it still bothers me."

*　　*　　*

"Maybe my parents' divorce has made me more protective of my own marriage. The very thought of divorce brings back a flood of unhappy memories. I was eleven at the time, and I never quite got over the feeling of being split in two. Even now I feel torn between my parents' families on holidays. Both of them act just a little hurt if my family and I go to the 'other's.' I've had a good life, and I don't think my childhood left me with any permanent damage, but I envy someone who has just one set of parents."

*　　*　　*

"My parents' divorce changed the course of my life," said Keith Harper. "Mom always struggled to keep us fed and dressed decently for school, while my father concentrated his efforts on his new family. He was plenty well off and could easily have helped send us to college, but my brother and I felt we had to go to work to help out mother. In the meantime my dad's stepdaughter and my two half-brothers went to the best schools and had all kinds of help getting started in business. The payoff was when he died and left everything to his second family. *Almost* everything. Jeff and I got five thou each—out of an estate worth millions."

* * *

"My blended family childhood was a pretty happy one. We were five teenagers, and I think we bonded as we shared the struggles of that age. I have a warm relationship with my older stepsister that began one afternoon when I came home and found her crying on the stairs. She'd taken our folks' car for a spin without permission and wrecked it, and she was so scared of what our parents would say. I remember feeling really special that she would confide in me."

Our Children's Memories

I asked our own children some hard questions. Do you remember how you felt about the divorce? About getting a stepparent? About moving? Were you sad, disappointed, angry? I prodded them with those kinds of questions and got some hard answers. A son-in-law said I had colossal nerve to ask our grown-up kids what they thought of their childhood.

Although I urged them to be honest, our sons and daughters are kind-hearted people, and I know they tempered their answers a bit. Even so, I am still reeling a little at the answers they gave.

Some of them were a surprise; some of them hurt. I wish I had been wise enough to have protected them from *their* hurt. It shows through between the lines they wrote. Some of their answers to the question, "How did you feel. . . ?" revealed a great deal of emotion.

"I don't remember being angry. I was more scared, not knowing what to expect."

"I know I wouldn't want my kids to experience what I did at seven or eight. Going through a divorce for a kid is more than sadness or anger. It's a sense of insecurity, a feeling of loss. I remember that vague sense of helplessness—being out of control of what was happening to me."

"It was a scary time for me. I felt rejected by my foster parents and displaced in my new family."

"I always hoped my original parents would be reunited and was upset when Dad told me the divorce was final. Even so, the prospect of getting a stepfamily was exciting."

"I was happy where I was and didn't want to leave."

"It was extremely difficult for me to adjust to my new home environment. I'd moved around to too many surrogate parents, and I was too confused and alienated to adjust."

"I wanted to be with my Dad but was torn about leaving my foster family. I was very close to them."

*   *   *

My question about our decision to move everyone away from familiar surroundings evoked these comments:

"It was a very positive move for me—a turning point in my life. A new beginning. I was excited about getting a stepsister, more than having a new stepmother."

"I understand your moving, but I don't think we should

have moved so far away from friends and familiar territory—and my father."

"Moving to Solvang was a good decision, especially for you and Dad. It was hard leaving friends, but easy to make new ones. Living in the country was a new experience, and there were plenty of places to explore. My 'new' brothers soon became my playmates to build forts or play army. It was kind of like going to camp."

"It all seemed like a great adventure. It helped us get to know each other. Since we didn't have friends to spend time with, we were forced to spend time with each other."

*   *   *

I remember how displaced and overwhelmed I felt that first night at the dinner table and for a long time afterwards. Everything was so strange. The kids weren't themselves either, but I didn't have the courage until now to ask them how they'd really felt.

"I felt isolated, in a way—things had changed so quickly. Someone I'd just met a few months ago was suddenly my brother and sharing a room with me."

"I felt like our family members were guests of your family at first."

"My relationship with you changed. With so many kids and a new husband, it was probably all you could do to keep up with the demands of cooking, cleaning, and laundry. You weren't able to spend much time with me at times when I might have needed it. But I think I understood your predicament and accepted it without any resentment."

"At first the idea of all those kids to play with was great. But it didn't work out so well. I never felt like I fit in."

"I remember the family going through some hard times.

Life got so tense in the house you asked me if I would rather go live with Dad. I was shocked that you would suggest it."

"With such a large family it was tough for you two to give individual attention to each kid. So the ones having the most problems would get the most attention."

"It was hard to go from having my own room to sharing with someone else and always having people around. I like the idea of big families, but I needed some space, too."

*   *   *

I didn't like the idea of our being a stepfamily. I never referred to myself as anyone's stepmother nor to any of the kids as stepchildren. I wanted us to be a nice, normal, "real" family. I asked the kids if we'd felt like one family or if they'd felt a division between us.

"Being part of a stepfamily was not uncomfortable at all. There were lots of stepfamilies when we were growing up. But yes, there was a division. Our side seemed to have more problems; our stepsiblings were more stable, better students. Living in a foster family was much more of a stigma than being in a stepfamily."

"I told my friends that our family was like the Brady Bunch."

"Because my dad remarried I am part of two stepfamilies. I'm often uncomfortable in his household, because I don't fit neatly into a role—'daughter' is well defined, but 'stepdaughter' is not. I'm not truly a member of the family there, but neither am I a guest. Probably the discomfort I still feel would have disappeared (as it did in my relationship with Dad, referring to Harry) if I had lived closer to my father's second family and worn the stepdaughter shoe more often."

"My advice to people undergoing blending (and unblending) is to remember that the members of the restructured family (in particular the children) are feeling their ways into new relationships without a clear picture of what it means to be a 'step' relation. Joan and I easily fell into sisterhood because we were friends first, and I'm sure that's how we really thought of each other for months and maybe even years after the blending. I think friend, caregiver, financial supporter, confidant, encourager, self-esteem booster, guide, etc. are all good starting points. Jumping into the relationship as parent (or daughter, sister, brother, for that matter) brings with it expectations which may be different for each person and can result in confusion and even resentment if these expectations aren't met. Let the parent do the parenting, and allow the stepparent to approach the relationship from a different, broader, less well-defined base."

"I never saw it as 'them' and 'us.' I think we did a remarkable job of becoming a family in such a short time. I consider Joan as my sister and my stepbrothers as brothers."

"I was not at all embarrassed about my blended family. We were an oddity, but I looked at it as being unique or special. If I envied 'normal' families, it was because they could do more as families. There were too many of us to go out to eat or on special outings."

*   *   *

To the question: "How about our asking you to call us Mom and Dad," I got these responses:

"I'd called others 'Mom' and 'Dad' before, so that wasn't hard for me. It made me feel more equal to call you 'Mom'."

"It was fine with me. I was young enough so that it wasn't a big deal. It made us more of a family, I think. I never felt there was a 'his kids' and 'her kids' kind of distinction. A lot of that was due to the fact that we all called you 'Mom' and 'Dad'."

"The only time it made me feel uncomfortable was when I referred to my stepfather as 'Dad' in front of my real dad."

"I remember being a little resistant to the idea at thirteen. Maybe it's not a good idea for older kids, since the stepparent can't really fill the role of parent at that late stage."

*   *   *

I really opened up a can of worms by asking what we should have done differently.

"It would have been nice to have had more touching and holding. I wish you'd had more time to spend with each individual. I never knew you as people. I learned more about you after leaving home than I ever knew about you living with you."

"I would have liked more encouragement in the things I did growing up. I think there should be more parent participation in what kids are doing and more individual attention."

"I felt that I got what I needed growing up. Materially, I had what my friends did, and that was what was important to me as a teenager. As a parent I'm glad I have more time to spend with each of my kids."

"I wish there had been less 'unblending' (of our original family). If there were anything I'd change, it would be the move. I wish our natural father had been more a part of our lives."

*   *   *

But there were some encouraging comments, as well:

"You did a great job, given a tough situation. Our family times centered around dinner, football games, picnics at Nojoqui Falls and the beach, and family friends. We hope to give our children similar experiences. We have added travel to that list, as well as extended family time that I think was missing from my childhood. But I don't think that was because we were a blended family. It was more a result of family personalities."

"I think I had a happy childhood. Growing up in a large family was a positive experience for me."

"There were many good times and some bad ones, but all in all they were happy times and I miss them. I miss the wry sarcasm among brothers and how comically brutal it could get. I miss sticking up for my little sister when someone picked on her (although she still says I never protected her) and getting the comfort or scoldings I needed from my big sister, who did both equally well. I miss my big brother, too, who more than once got me out of a precarious situation. I miss the football games in the backyard (We couldn't have done that in a small family!) and exploring the back fields with all my brothers and sisters."

"Yes, I miss it all—the struggles and laughs and ups and downs. Blended or not, our family was built on love and nurtured with patience, and that is what family is all about. I may have some regrets, but I wouldn't change a thing."

"I think you and Dad gave us a great example of what a good marital relationship could be."

*   *   *

The answers to the questions, "How did you see us as parents? Did you feel loved? Were we too strict or not strict enough?" could very well have come from children of nuclear families.

"You did a very good job as parents. I could count on you both. You weren't strict, but we had limitations, which were important."

"I think you tried very hard to be fair. As a parent now, I realize that sometimes it's impossible to be fair. But as I recall, you tried, and that's what's important. If you were partial to some of us, I think it was because they'd earned your trust and extra privileges. In my teenage years you expected me to make good choices, so I did without a whole lot of involvement from you. I had a solid foundation from early childhood upon which to base my decisions in later childhood."

"If a child's parents get mad at him for doing something wrong, and then the child sees the brother being praised for doing something right, it may appear to the 'bad' child that the 'good' one is being favored. But it probably isn't so. I think we were treated fairly, but some of us (including me) messed up more than others."

"I learned a lot of values that I still hold true today."

"I tried to find my place in the family but felt like an outcast. I don't think it was just this family but something I'd always felt. Most of the time I felt my presence made little difference one way or the other."

"You weren't always fair, but it evened out. I didn't feel unconditionally loved. I felt I had to earn your love."

"Though we all lived together, we seemed to act as individuals instead of as a family. We cared about each other, but we cared about ourselves more."

"I recall a general feeling of being out-of-touch, alienated. I felt loved, but in a distant, unapproachable sort of way."

"I know some of my siblings didn't *like* me, but I guess I felt loved, at least by my parents."

*　　*　　*

"Were there any advantages of growing up in a blended family?" I asked them. I think their answers to this last question indicate that they gained at least as much as they lost.

"I learned to adapt to change. As an adult this trait has allowed me to face a crisis more easily than I may have otherwise. Living with a large family has helped me in dealing with people, too. I can accept people the way they are.''

"I feel concern for children other than my own biological children. I saw five of my siblings coming from foster homes— homes that had a significant impact on the early lives of these children. I think this is the reason I'm a foster parent today.''

"I'm probably more accepting of other people and their differences. I'm not too idealistic. But I have a problem with self-esteem. I think that may come from the upheaval during my childhood.''

"I learned to be thrifty. There are a lot of things we can do without, even if we think we need them. 'Things' are not very important to me. Growing up, I found that love was more important than things. That value has stayed with me.''

*   *   *

Our children's words help us to understand them, as I hope this book may help them to better understand us. But I wrote it for you, the reader, to warn you of some of the pitfalls and encourage you by some of the joys that can be found in blended families. You may be encouraged, as I have been, by this statement by Edith Schaeffer:

> What is a family? A family is a mobile. A family is the most versatile, ever-changing mobile that exists. . . . A mobile is a moving, changing collection of objects constantly in motion, yet within the framework of a form. The framework of a family gives form, but as one starts with a man and woman, a mother and father, there is never any one day following another when these two, plus the children that come through adoption or birth into the home, are either the same age or at the same point of growth. Every individual is growing, changing, developing, or declining—intellectually, emotionally, spiritually, physically, and psychologically. A

family is a grouping of individuals who are *affecting* each other intellectually, emotionally, spiritually, physically, psychologically. No two years, no two months, or no two days is there the exact same blend or mix within the family, as each individual person is changing.[1]

12
The Reunion

*O*ver the rooftops of Aspen Lodge, beyond the lake and the meadow and across the winding highway, Long's Peak rises from the deep green of the pine forest, thrusting upward against a sweep of blue Colorado sky. Above the timberline a lace cap of snow, shrinking in these first warm days of summer, sparkles in the early afternoon sun.

Harry and I have come up to our cabin after lunch to relax and read a little, leaving the others to go their own ways. Now Harry has fallen asleep over Louis L'Amour, and I have come out to sit on the cabin step and drink in the delicious Rocky Mountain air.

Below me and to the left of the lodge the young men vie for victory in the horseshoe pit. Metal clanks against metal, and there is a cheer and a protest and a guffaw. Tom plays with one arm, because his other is in a sling. I cringe as I remember his tumble down the lodge steps on our second day here. His laughter is a thin covering for his pain and disappointment.

Splish, splash from the pool area, and I see young mothers with their little ones. The delighted squeals come from Katie and Carrie. "Mommy, catch me! Here I come!" Nancy opens arms wide for her daughters.

"C'mon, Louis, watch me swim! Look now, I'm staying up!" Christopher shouts for his cousin's attention. I remember a sterile nursery, seven years ago, and a tiny preemie struggling for life.

Four-year-old Daniel heads for the swings, and Mike runs to give him a push. "Me, too, Uncle Mike!" Jeff yells, racing across the lawn to join them.

Flecks of color blend with the tall grass near the lake and move into focus to reveal a family fishing. Gold tee shirts tell me it is Chris and his older boys. Frances and Joseph are at the pool.

The tee shirts are a surprise gift from Joan and Laurie, bubbling with excited anticipation as they present them at dinner. Twenty-seven shirts, custom-made, ranging from little Erik's size one to Kathy's maternity model. Each family unit has a different color, and on the front are the words PREFAB FAMILY, COLORADO '84 and an outline drawing of the old house where we all grew up. "Look," Kenny tells the waiter, "you can tell who belongs to who by our colors." The tall young waiter is on his knees to take orders from the little kids, grouped at one round table by their foolhardy parents, who have gathered for adult conversation at another.

"Don't you think someone should be watching them?" Harry asks me, eyeing a stemmed water goblet that teeters precariously close to the edge of the table, as Jeffrey bounces into his place between Katie and Daniel. Eight-year-old Joseph has seniority at the little kids' table. Erik and Carrie are secure in high chairs beside their parents, and the teens and older kids—Gina, Linc, Craig, and Kenny—sit with the adults. At the next meal there will be a shifting of seats. There is only a week for everyone to talk to everyone.

"Family pictures at three o'clock!" Laurie announces, coming from the kitchen, where she has borrowed a tripod from one of the staff. "Don't forget!"

We are missing a few of us. Steve, of course. And Mark and Venita and little Anna. It won't be a whole family, in spite of careful planning. "Next time," someone says, "you should send out orders with the invitations, forbidding unauthorized pregnancies." There is a chorus of good-natured grumbles as we think of Venita in her final month. Kathy blushes and tugs at her maternity top.

"Uncle Harry! Shoot some baskets?" It's Linc, tired of fishing, coming up from the lake with a basketball. Harry holds his hands above his head for the catch and then turns, smooth as a ballet dancer, to sail the ball in a graceful arc toward the hoop. "Hey, Craig, wanta play?" Linc calls to his cousin, his adolescent voice cracking. "Watch Uncle Harry!"

Uncle Harry, grown straight and tall and handsome. "He's graduated from college, you know," his father says proudly at every opportunity. "Has his degree in journalism now." I am proud, too.

Through the aspen leaves that shade our cabin I glimpse two blond heads, close together. Erik bounces in the baby carrier on his father's back, as Greg strides toward the stables. He turns to wave at Kathy, stretched out on a lounge by the pool. They smile love at each other.

Kristi comes down the steps of their cabin, and Tom leaves the game of horseshoes to join her. They wave to Louis and walk over to the pool, arm in arm. I wonder if they're remembering how they met, at Young Life Camp in Canada. Tom's leg was in a cast then, the result of his first attempt at water skiing. Kristi's compassion attracted him then, sustains him now.

Terre and Dave and Mike are in conversation as they gather the horseshoes from the dusty pit. Dave points to his new station wagon in front of their cabin, and the others look up and nod enthusiastically. Sons-in-law, extenders of the family circle, enrichers of my life.

The click of the cabin door makes me glance over my shoulder. Harry has come out to sit beside me. "It's been a great week, hasn't it?" he asks, knowing my answer.

"Wonderful. You know where it says in the Bible that God will give us the desires of our hearts, if we delight ourselves in Him?"

"That's in Psalms, isn't it?"

"Yes. Well, there were two things I desired that I thought were out of reach forever. I always thought that if we'd had a baby together it would make our marriage more valid. Sitting here, looking out at these precious grandchildren of ours, I realize that God has compensated us many times over for that lack."

"And the other wish?"

"In the midst of all the havoc, when the kids were growing up, I thought we'd made such a mistake. I wished somehow that it could come out all right. It has."

Notes

CHAPTER ONE

1. Ruth Roosevelt and Jeanette Lofas, *Living in Step* (Stein and Day, 1976), p. 19.
2. Dr. Fitzhugh Dodson, *How to Discipline With Love: From Crib to College* (New York: Rawson Associates Publishers, Inc., 1977), p. 63.
3. John Hagedorn, "The Second Family," *The Lutheran* (May 15, 1985), pp. 12–14.

CHAPTER TWO

1. Carole Streeter, *Finding Your Place After Divorce: How Women Can Find Healing* (Grand Rapids: Zondervan Publishing House, 1986), pp. 42–43.
2. Amy Ross Mumford, *By Death or Divorce, It Hurts to Lose* (Denver: Accent Publications, Inc., 1976), pp. 122–3.
3. Morton Hunt, *The World of the Formerly Married* (New York: McGraw-Hill, 1966), p. 203.

CHAPTER THREE

1. Dwight Hervey Small, *Design for Christian Marriage* (Old Tappan: Fleming H. Revell Company, 1975), pp. 136–7.
2. Norman Wright, *The Fulfilled Marriage* (Irvine, Calif.: Harvest House Publishers, 1976), p. 17.

CHAPTER FOUR

1. Elizabeth Einstein, *The Stepfamily: Living, Loving and Learning* (New York: Macmillan, 1982), p. 127.
2. John Hagedorn, "The Second Family," pp. 12–14.

CHAPTER FIVE

1. Gladys M. Hunt, "Guidelines to Happy Families," *Raising a Joyful Family* (New York: Harper and Row, 1983), p. 10. (This originally appeared in *Moody Monthly*, reprinted by *The Christian Reader*.)

2. Dwight Hervey Small, *Design for Christian Marriage*, p. 18.

3. Jeanne Thompson Varnell, "Blended Family Concerns," *Christian Home* (1983–84), p. 41.

4. Tom and Adrienne Frydenger, *The Blended Family* (Grand Rapids: Zondervan Publishing House, 1986), p. 15.

5. Richard B. Stuart and Barbara Jacobson, *Second Marriage—Make it Happy! Make it Last!* (New York: W.W. Norton, 1985), p. 64.

6. Dwight Hervey Small, *Design for Christian Marriage*, p. 18.

CHAPTER SIX

1. Charles Swindoll, *Dropping Your Guard* (Waco: Word, Inc., 1983), p. 122.

2. Joyce Landorf, *Changepoints* (Old Tappan: Fleming H. Revell, 1981), pp. 50–51.

3. D. Ross Campbell, M.D., *How to Really Love Your Child* (Wheaton: Victor Books, 1977), p. 32.

4. Dennis Guernsey, *If I'm So Free How Come I Feel Boxed In?* (Waco: Word, Inc. 1978), p. 17.

CHAPTER SEVEN

1. Dr. James Dobson, *Dare to Discipline* (Wheaton: Tyndale House Publishers, Inc., 1970), p. 77.

2. Benjamin Spock, M.D., "Can One Parent Be As Good As Two?", *Redbook* (April 1987), p. 17.

3. C.S. Lewis, *The Four Basic Loves* (New York: Harcourt Brace Jovanavich, 1960).